Business
and Industry

EDITORS

William R. Childs
Scott B. Martin
Wanda Stitt-Gohdes

VOLUME 10

TEMPORARY WORKERS to
YAMAHA CORPORATION

MARSHALL CAVENDISH
NEW YORK · TORONTO · LONDON · SYDNEY

Marshall Cavendish
99 White Plains Road
Tarrytown, New York 10591-9001

www.marshallcavendish.com

© 2004 Marshall Cavendish Corporation

Library of Congress Cataloging-in-Publication Data

Business and industry / editors, William R. Childs, Scott B. Martin, Wanda Stitt-Gohdes.
      p. cm.
    Includes bibliographical reference and index.
    Contents: v. 1. Accounting and Bookkeeping to Burnett, Leo--v. 2. Business Cycles to Copyright--v. 3. Corporate Governance to Entrepreneurship--v. 4. Environmentalism to Graham, Katharine--v. 5. Great Depression to Internship--v. 6. Inventory to Merrill Lynch--. v. 7. Microeconomics to Philip Morris Companies--v. 8. Price Controls to Sarnoff, David--v. 9. Savings and Investment Options to Telecommuting--v. 10. Temporary Workers to Yamaha--v. 11. Index volume
    ISBN 0-7614-7430-7 (set)--ISBN 0-7614-7440-4 (v. 10)
      1. Business--Encyclopedias. 2. Industries--Encyclopedias. I. Childs, William R., 1951-II. Martin, Scott B., 1961-III. Stitt-Gohdes, Wanda.

HF1001 .B796 2003
338'.003--dc21   2002035156

Printed in Italy

06 05 04 03 5 4 3 2 1

MARSHALL CAVENDISH
Editorial Director   Paul Bernabeo
Production Manager   Alan Tsai

Produced by The Moschovitis Group, Inc.

THE MOSCHOVITIS GROUP
President, Publishing Division   Valerie Tomaselli
Executive Editor   Hilary W. Poole
Associate Editor   Sonja Matanovic
Design and Layout   Annemarie Redmond
Illustrator   Richard Garratt
Assistant Illustrator   Zahiyya Abdul-Karim
Photo Research   Gillian Speeth
Production Associates   K. Nura Abdul-Karim, Rashida Allen
Editorial Assistants   Christina Campbell, Nicole Cohen, Jessica Rosin
Copyediting   Carole Campbell
Proofreading   Paul Scaramazza
Indexing   AEIOU, Inc.

Alphabetical Table of Contents

PHOTO CREDITS:

Temporary Workers

Originally, temporary workers provided short-term clerical help or manual labor; temporary work has evolved to include the practice of leasing employees for long-term projects. The turnover rate of this contingent workforce is about 400 percent per year, most of it attributable to the shorter-term "temp" workers. Although the perception that the United States will become a nation of contingent workers is widespread, in 1998 less than 5 percent of jobs were held by the contingent workforce, according to a 1999 survey by the Labor Department's Bureau of Labor Statistics.

Kinds of Temporary Work

Temporary workers can be found throughout the whole economic structure. Many companies and businesses use temporary workers for a variety of jobs in areas like manufacturing, agriculture, maintenance, clerical, technology, service, and so on. Historically, temporary work consisted of the primarily blue-collar jobs that involved manual labor in farming and manufacturing or the so-called pink-collar jobs involving clerical work. With the technology explosion of the 1990s, longer-term temporary work became available in the white-collar world of business as well.

There are as many kinds of work arrangements as there are kinds of temporary workers. Temporary jobs can be part-time, on-call, day labor, short-term, or contract. Some of the work is seasonal, for example, the hiring of migrant workers for harvest in agriculture, extra sales associates during the holidays in retail, or extra accountants during tax season. Temporary workers are also called on during periods of increased workloads, during transitions, and to fill in for employees on leave of absence. Longer-term temps, sometimes called permatemps, usually work on a project basis for a specified period.

Workers get involved in temporary jobs for a variety of reasons. Some people do temp work as a way of life. Others—students, teachers, or mothers of young children—may do temp work for supplemental income. Still others use temp work to tide them over while looking for a new job. These workers often look for temp firms that have "temp-to-perm" arrangements, where a temporary assignment can lead to a full-time job.

One company that depends on temps is United Parcel Service (UPS). At one point, UPS studied the high turnover rate of its delivery truck drivers. The drivers' two basic tasks were to load the truck and to deliver packages. UPS found that the drivers did not like the tedious job of loading their trucks. As learning a route is more time-consuming than learning to load a truck, UPS created a new position: truck loaders. UPS often uses seasonal temps and students to fill these positions because the training period is so short.

Staffing Firms

Many temporary workers are hired through staffing firms, which are of two main kinds: temp agencies and contracting firms. Each has a slightly different focus and serves a different segment of the working community.

Temp firms typically hire people who will work for companies for short periods to fill a very specific need. Temps fill out an application to register with the service, then are "on call" for available jobs. Temps are

See also:
Contracts and Contract Law; Human Resources; Technology.

Contrary to widespread impressions, the percentage of workers in so-called alternate arrangements, including temporary work, is not large and did not increase in the 1990s.

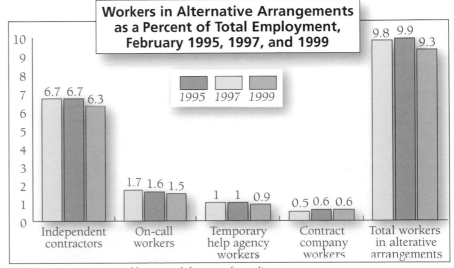

Workers in Alternative Arrangements as a Percent of Total Employment, February 1995, 1997, and 1999

1995   1997   1999

Independent contractors: 6.7 6.7 6.3
On-call workers: 1.7 1.6 1.5
Temporary help agency workers: 1 1 0.9
Contract company workers: 0.5 0.6 0.6
Total workers in alterative arrangements: 9.8 9.9 9.3

Note: Components may not add up to totals because of rounding.
Source: Bureau of Labor Statistics, http://www.bls.gov/opub/ted/2001/apr/wk4/art03.htm (March 18, 2003).

Many offices employ temporary workers to perform clerical work.

usually paid per job, and they may or may not receive benefits from the temp firm. Often, a business can call a temp service and get help that same day.

Contract firms provide longer-term help, usually on a project basis. They hire people in one of two ways. The first is similar to a temp agency: workers submit their resumes and are called when a job is available. If workers work overtime, they are paid overtime by the hour. These workers may or may not qualify for benefits.

The second is to hire workers as salaried employees of the contract firm. As in other salaried positions, these workers do not get overtime pay. These workers are given full benefits through the contract firm, and when they finish a job, the contract firm will usually continue to pay them while they "sit on the bench" until they are contracted out again. If no jobs are available for that person after a set time, then the contract firm can lay him or her off.

Contract firms gained a high profile during the technology boom of the 1990s. Two trends converged to create the ideal environment for contract work. Previously, there had been more people than jobs; suddenly the technology sector had more jobs than qualified people. The environment of fierce competition that ensued found companies outbidding one another to get qualified workers. People would jump from company to company as the salaries increased.

Contract firms gave top-quality technical people the freedom to move around without incurring the stigma of being a job hopper. Hired out on a project basis, if a more lucrative project became available at the current project's end, the contractor was free to move on. Contract firms also allowed businesses to take on additional employees for short periods with little or no risk. The companies could release contractors without the costs attached to laying off employees.

Contract firms provide a key benefit to both employees and employers. They serve as a kind of human resources department. For the employee, they provide benefits and forward payroll taxes to the government. For the employer, they have already performed all the recruiting, screening, and interviewing functions that are so time-consuming, especially in a hot job market. The employer pays the contract firm a set amount for certain kinds of employees, then the contract firm provides that number of people with that skill level. An interesting legal development is the trend of courts to treat the employer and the contract firm as co-employers. This makes them legally jointly responsible for employment responsibilities, for example, taxes and working conditions.

Independent Contractors and Guest Workers

Independent contractors make up another segment of the contingent workforce. They provide either short- or long-term expertise to a company in a hands-on manner. (This contrasts with consultants, who typically function as advisers rather than development or production team members.) They are self-employed and handle all human resources functions themselves, including finding jobs, paying taxes, and negotiating wages. Legal guidelines define who can be considered an independent contractor. These guidelines address, among other issues, who controls the employee's workplace, hours, and assessment of performance. Independent contractors typically work on a project basis and rely heavily on networking and advertising to find new jobs.

Nonimmigrants from foreign countries who apply for and receive permission to work in the United States are sometimes called "guest workers." They travel to the United States seeking short-term employment, some with the hope of gaining permanent residency. Some of these workers are educated and have specific skills, for example, those entering on an H-1B visa to work in the computer industry. They work for several years on a renewable visa.

Others, particularly those from Mexico, come to the United States on short-term work visas for seasonal work. These workers are usually paid very low wages; however, the wage is often greater than what they could earn in their home countries. Accordingly, they may look for ways to remain in the United States—sometimes legally, other times illegally.

Issues in Temporary Work

The question of benefits generates the greatest source of dissatisfaction for temp workers. Because the average length of employment for temp workers is four to six months, many staffing firms find offering benefits impractical. By the time the person qualifies for benefits, he or she is usually ready to move on.

Two other factors can make temp jobs undesirable. Contingent work offers little job security. Some employers have decided to protect themselves against future economic crises by creating a temporary workforce within their ranks. Temp workers can be released for performance, when the economy takes a downturn, or for many other reasons.

Wages for temp workers are typically below what their full-time counterparts earn. For people who are unemployed, temp jobs will most likely disqualify them from receiving unemployment benefits.

Seasonal workers harvest lettuce in California's San Joaquin Valley in 1989.

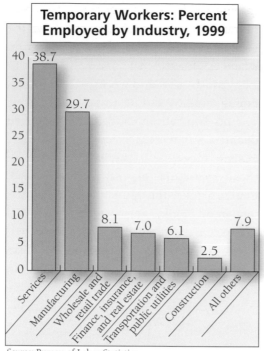

Temporary Workers: Percent Employed by Industry, 1999

- Services: 38.7
- Manufacturing: 29.7
- Wholesale and retail trade: 8.1
- Finance, insurance, and real estate: 7.0
- Transportation and public utilities: 6.1
- Construction: 2.5
- All others: 7.9

Source: Bureau of Labor Statistics, http://www.bls.gov/opub/ted/2001/apr/wk5/art03.txt (March 18, 2003).

Currently very few labor laws protect temporary workers from abuses in the system. One example of how lawsuits are helping define the rules is the case of *Microsoft Corp. v. Vizcaino*, filed in 1992. The lawsuit was settled in 2000 when the federal courts found Microsoft guilty of misclassifying employees as independent contractors. Microsoft was required to compensate thousands of workers for benefits they should have received, such as cut-rate stock purchases.

Organized labor advocates take issue with the idea that flexibility for the company must necessarily mean insecurity for the worker. A ruling by the National Labor Relations Board in September 2000 made forming organized bargaining units easier for temps. Temporary workers can now join unions and reap the rewards of bargaining with management for rights and benefits. Businesses generally take a dim view of this development because it could mean that both staffing firms and workers have a say in the contract negotiations, instead of just the staffing firm. White-collar temps are unlikely to be affected; blue- and pink-collar workers stand to gain the most. Many of these are women working in garment manufacturing, clerical positions, and service jobs.

The Future

Because very few legal boundaries have been set for contingent workers, many parties interested in labor relations are beginning to push for laws that protect them. Portable benefits are one possibility, or the creation of associations where members can gain access to health benefits. Labor activists are working for new laws that ensure equal wages and equal benefits for the same work performed by temps and permanent workers.

Other kinds of temp work and contract arrangements have begun to emerge in the white-collar sector. For example, bigger computer services companies, including EDS and IBM, outsource their employees to smaller companies. In the 1990s temp jobs for CEOs emerged as the dot-com explosion lured experienced executives away from larger corporations. Temp CEOs have a special role: when they come into a company, they have full power to make decisions at all levels, including financial, resource allocation, and firing. Their challenge is to make sound business decisions without alienating long-term employees.

These and other niche opportunities indicate that the business world will continue to change to meet the needs of individuals as well as companies. The United States may never become a nation of contingent workers, but the flexibility of a contingent workforce in a world of ever-increasing complexity offers the perfect opportunity for those in transition, those with skills in high demand, and those who need a little extra income.

Further Reading

Barker, Kathleen, and Kathleen Christensen, eds. *Contingent Work: American Employment Relations in Transition.* New York: Cornell University Press, 1998.

Damico, Joan. *How to Be a Permanent Temp: Winning Strategies for Thriving in Today's Workplace.* Franklin Lakes, N.J.: Career Press, 2001.

Woods, Saralee T. *Executive Temping: A Guide for Professionals.* New York: John Wiley & Sons, 1998.

—*Stephanie Buckwalter*

Texaco

In 1859 at Oil Creek in Titusville, Pennsylvania, Edwin Drake and William A. Smith used a new method, drilling, to bring oil to the surface. Their discovery triggered an oil rush as fortune seekers rushed to buy land and construct oil derricks. By 1880 John D. Rockefeller and his company, Standard Oil, controlled more than 90 percent of the oil refining in the United States, leaving very little room for competitors. However, in 1901 a new oil field was tapped at Spindletop Hill, outside Beaumont, Texas. These fields would prove to be far larger than previous finds, and within two years more than 500 oil firms had flocked to Texas. One of the most successful of these was the Texas Oil Company.

The find at Spindletop coincided with a huge shift in the use of oil. Up to that time, most oil had been refined into kerosene and used for heating. With the invention of the gasoline-powered internal combustion engine, gasoline became a much more important oil product.

The Texas Oil Company was founded in 1902 by Joe "Buckskin" Cullinan, an oil veteran who had formerly worked for Standard, and Arnold Schlaet, a New York investor. Their fledgling oil firm hit black gold in Sour Lake Field, also in Texas, just a year later. Although Standard Oil was a very powerful company, the sheer number of firms in the early years of the twentieth century thwarted Standard's policy of attempting to control all of them. Although the newer firms were tiny compared with Standard, Schlaet had invested $3 million in Texas Oil, enough to ensure that the company was competitive.

Not long after the Sour Lake discovery, the firm erected its first refinery, at Port Arthur, Texas. In 1907 the company changed its name to Texaco and began an extensive retail and marketing network. Texaco also developed a new, continuous refining process that dramatically boosted gasoline yields. Within a decade, Texaco was running tanker operations up and down the East Coast and refining operations as far inland as Illinois.

Foreign Oil

The breakup of Standard in 1911 opened the field even wider for new oil companies. Texaco was quick to take advantage of these opportunities and was one of the first to realize the potential in exploiting foreign oil fields.

As the early oil fields in Texas started to become depleted, oil companies began casting around for foreign oil fields. In

See also:
Bankruptcy; Multinational Corporation; Organization of Petroleum Exporting Countries; Standard Oil.

A magazine advertisement for Texaco from the early twentieth century.

The corrosion test assures freedom from corrosive deposits in the gas line and carburetor. A little strip of polished copper is immersed in heated Texaco Gasoline. Not a trace of tarnish is permitted. Texaco chemists, with hundreds of daily tests, certify the quality of Texaco.

On the long trail
with Texaco

THE TEXACO RED STAR AND GREEN T is always with you or just ahead. You are never far from that old, familiar sign.

There you can get Texaco, the volatile gas, with its pick-up, power and mileage; and Texaco, the clean, clear, golden oil—and know what you're getting.

Up and over the scenic trail through a wonderful country on a wonderful day. Texaco carries you safely and surely.

The long trail is a short trail with Texaco in the tank—and the clean, clear, golden Texaco Motor Oil in the crankcase easing the way.

THE TEXAS COMPANY, U. S. A.
Texaco Petroleum Products

TEXACO
GASOLINE MOTOR OIL

Persia (now Iran) the British government formed the Anglo-Persian Oil Company. Other oil producers established their spheres of influence. In Saudi Arabia, Standard of California (Socal, now Chevron) and Texaco formed the Arab-American Oil Company (Aramco) in 1936. At the same time, Texaco purchased 50 percent of Bahrain Petroleum and, together with Socal, formed the California-Texas Oil Company (Caltex) as an outlet for future oil production in Bahrain and Saudi Arabia. Texaco was also involved in large oil ventures in Indonesia and Venezuela.

Throughout the 1930s and 1940s, a great deal of backroom maneuvering took place between oil-exporting countries and the foreign companies that possessed the technology for exploration, the financial resources for processing, and the distribution network. In 1950 Aramco and Saudi Arabia hammered out a new accord based on the 50–50 principle: for a lump-sum royalty paid to producers, plus a 50–50 split in profits, oil companies like Aramco could purchase drilling and export rights. The agreement became the standard, allowing oil companies like Texaco to continue their foreign operations while the foreign governments received a share of the profits.

Although Texas remained an important source of oil for Texaco, the company continued to develop extensive production areas in the Gulf of Mexico, Saudi Arabia, Asia, the Caribbean, and West Africa. Eventually, the company became involved in oil production and sales in more than 150 countries. Texaco grew to become one of the "seven sisters," a name given to the seven companies that dominated the world oil industry.

Texaco geologists using 3-D imaging software to look for oil (undated photo).

Legal Catastrophe

In 1984 Pennzoil and Getty Oil agreed to a merger. Before the merger was finalized, Texaco offered Getty a substantially better deal. Getty Oil reneged on the Pennzoil deal and merged with Texaco instead. Pennzoil immediately sued Texaco, claiming that Texaco had illegally interfered in the negotiations. Pennzoil won the case and was awarded $11.1 billion, the largest judgment in the United States to that time. Texaco appealed; a Texas appeals court later reduced the judgment to $9 billion, but interest and penalties drove it up to $10.3 billion.

Texaco offered Pennzoil $2 billion to settle, but Pennzoil demanded between $3 billion and $5 billion. In April 1987, just days before Pennzoil began to file liens against Texaco's assets, Texaco declared bankruptcy. While appealing the judgment against it, Texaco had been required to post a $12 billion bond. By filing for bankruptcy under Chapter 11, Texaco also avoided having to post the bond. Within hours of the bankruptcy declaration, Texaco and Pennzoil struck a deal for $3 billion. Texaco emerged from bankruptcy the same day and was back in business.

Texaco then underwent a massive restructuring, including sales of assets and the formation of the Star Enterprise joint-venture partnership with the Saudi Arabian Oil Company. Although Texaco recovered from the Pennzoil suit, other large lawsuits followed. In 1996 Texaco agreed to pay $176 million to settle a racial discrimination suit brought by employees; since 1993 Texaco has been fighting a lawsuit brought by a group of Ecuadorean Indians who filed an action in U.S. federal court accusing the company of environmental negligence.

The combination of problems left Texaco with insufficient profits but considerable resources, making it ripe for a takeover. At the end of 2000 Chevron purchased Texaco for $35 billion, creating the world's fifth largest oil company (after ExxonMobil, Royal Dutch/Shell, BP Amoco, and TotalFinaElf). The merger created a firm with a combined market value of $90 billion.

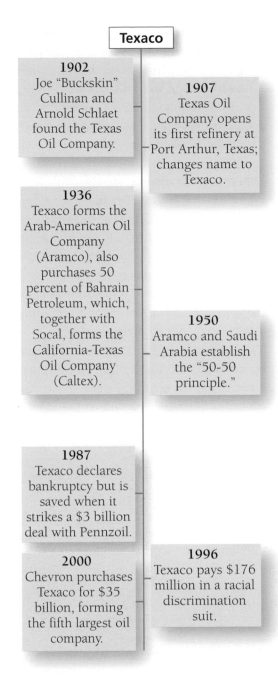

Texaco

1902
Joe "Buckskin" Cullinan and Arnold Schlaet found the Texas Oil Company.

1907
Texas Oil Company opens its first refinery at Port Arthur, Texas; changes name to Texaco.

1936
Texaco forms the Arab-American Oil Company (Aramco), also purchases 50 percent of Bahrain Petroleum, which, together with Socal, forms the California-Texas Oil Company (Caltex).

1950
Aramco and Saudi Arabia establish the "50-50 principle."

1987
Texaco declares bankruptcy but is saved when it strikes a $3 billion deal with Pennzoil.

1996
Texaco pays $176 million in a racial discrimination suit.

2000
Chevron purchases Texaco for $35 billion, forming the fifth largest oil company.

Further Reading

Delaney, Kevin. *Strategic Bankruptcy: How Corporations and Creditors Use Chapter 11 to Their Advantage.* Berkeley: University of California Press, 1999.

Economides, Michael, and Ronald Oligney. *The Color of Oil: The History, the Money, and the Politics of the World's Biggest Business.* Lanham, Md.: Lone Star Books, 2000.

Petzinger, Thomas, and Thomas Petzinger, Jr. *Oil and Honor: The Texaco-Pennzoil Wars.* Chevy Chase, Md.: Beard Books, 1999.

Roberts, Bari-Ellen. *Roberts vs. Texaco: A True Story of Race and Corporate America.* New York: Avon Books, 1998.

—*Lisa Magloff*

See also:

Competition; Customer
Service; ISO 9000;
Management Theory.

Total Quality Management

Total Quality Management (TQM) is a body of organizational and business theories and techniques that focus on ways to provide high-quality products and services. Its origin lies in the unpleasant discovery by U.S. businesses in the 1970s that products from several other countries, especially Japan and Germany, were superior in performance and overall quality to similar goods produced domestically. TQM concepts are the product of this awakening; although originally applied to the manufacture of large products like automobiles, they can be applied to businesses that produce both other products and services and to virtually all other forms of formal organization, including government, education, social

In 1994 an auto chassis is pulled from the assembly line at a Ford Motor Company plant for inspection by a quality control expert.

service, and so on. In essence, the key insights of TQM are the importance of quality at the source, continuous improvement of process, and striving to exceed the needs of the customer or user.

At the end of World War II, the United States was the world's only economic superpower. The deprivations of the Great Depression and the war had left so much pent-up demand for consumer goods that quantity and marketability were far more important than quality. As the economies of war-devastated nations were rebuilt, they needed to find ways to make their products competitive with those of the United States. They frequently chose quality as a primary competitive tool. U.S. businesses began to discover that they would have to compete on quality, too.

American businesses were inclined to view quality as an afterthought. They believed that consumers were primarily concerned

with product availability. Businesses also believed that product defects could be satisfactorily addressed after the fact. This created a tendency toward what is called produce-and-inspect (inspection by the company after production) and sell-and-fix (inspection by the customer after purchase), an economically inefficient way to create products. The waste in producing and selling defective and poor-quality goods was nevertheless ignored. As more and more firms began to lose out to foreign competition in the 1970s, the failure to produce high-quality goods initially could no longer be tolerated.

Economic competition forced on U.S. business this insight: in the long run doing something right the first time is more economically efficient. In addition to the embarrassing discovery that the rebuilt economies of America's wartime enemies were outshining and outdistancing U.S. businesses, an additional embarrassment was the discovery that many of the so-called new quality philosophies and techniques had already been developed by Americans—Philip B. Crosby, Joseph M. Juran, and W. Edwards Deming—but had been ignored by American companies.

Crosby, with wide industry experience in quality management, was an author, trainer, and consultant. His approach to quality emphasized eliminating failures and defects from all processes, with the ultimate goal being zero defects. This goal requires absolute commitment on the part of management to quality improvement, development of quality awareness throughout the organization, taking action to define and correct problems, instituting and sustaining training, and rigorous awareness of costs, particularly the costs of poor quality.

Juran's message was to apply quality concepts and methods throughout an organization using a broad-based system of components and interactions both internally and in external business relationships. He also argued that quality concerns require a beyond-the-company approach that includes consideration of customer needs and desires as well as supplier performance and capabilities.

Deming is the most famous philosopher of TQM (see box on p. 1310). He is so respected by the Japanese that they have named their major quality award for him. Despite his record of accomplishment and fame in Japan, he was relatively unknown in the United States until his concepts were presented in a 1980 television documentary. The central focus of Deming's ideas is stated in his concept of "profound knowledge," which has four components:

- Understanding of the concept of a system (the components and processes in interaction)
- Knowledge of the concept of variation and statistics (distinguishing between common causes of variation, which result from system design, and special causes, which lie in the behavior of individuals)

W. Edwards Deming

W. Edwards Deming, a statistician and business consultant, is widely considered to be the father of Total Quality Management. Born in Sioux City, Iowa, in 1900, Deming received a doctorate in physics at Yale in 1928. While attending Yale, he worked at the Western Electric Company under Walter Shewhart and came to study and admire Shewhart's theories on quality control in factories. From 1928 to 1945 Deming worked as a mathematician in various branches of the U.S. government.

After World War II, Deming traveled the world, helping to rebuild the economies of several war-torn countries. Deming's theories had their greatest impact in Japan. His philosophy, combined with his statistical models for improving quality control, had a profound effect on the thinking of Japan's business community and helped shape the corporate culture of the entire country. Many observers believe that the application of Deming's theories was largely responsible for Japan's astonishing postwar success. By the 1980s companies around the world were studying Deming's techniques, and even large American corporations, which had scorned and ignored his methods, now eagerly sought his advice.

Deming remained an active proponent and teacher of his philosophy until his death in 1993. His work is now carried on by the W. Edwards Deming Institute.

—*Colleen Sullivan*

Although originally developed for manufacturing, many TQM concepts, for example, the team-based approach to tasks, are applicable to many kinds of businesses.

- A theory of knowledge (knowledge as pragmatic understanding that is subject to revision based on testing and experimentation; not a list of absolutes)
- Understanding of human psychology (rooted in self-actualization psychology and related to worker empowerment and pride in work)

Understanding and implementation of these concepts is, to Deming, absolutely necessary for transforming organizations into effective systems that promote and constantly seek improvement, resulting in continually exceeding the expectations of customers. Businesses committed to TQM will experience customer satisfaction, high sales and profits, and will secure the future of the organization. Perhaps the most interesting aspect of Deming's philosophy is the fact that he never used the term *total quality management* nor did he promote it. Nevertheless, advocates of TQM will usually point to Deming as its originator and promulgator.

Further Reading

Crosby, Philip B. *Quality without Tears*. New York: McGraw-Hill, 1984.

Deming, W. Edwards. *The New Economics: For Industry, Government, Education*. Cambridge, Mass.: MIT Press, 1993.

Juran, Joseph M., ed. *A History of Managing for Quality: The Evolution, Trends, and Future Direction of Managing for Quality*. Milwaukee, Wis.: ASQC Quality Press, 1996.

Pegels, C. Carl. *Total Quality Management: A Survey of Its Important Aspects*. Boston, Mass.: Course Technology, 1994.

Walton, Mary. *The Deming Management Method*. New York: Dodd, Mead, 1986.

—*John Washbush*

Tourism Industry

The tourism industry is often ranked as the world's largest industry, providing nearly 255 million jobs, or almost 11 percent of the global workforce. It plays a vital role in the economies of at least 70 percent of the world's nations. Although Western countries, the United States, France, Spain, Italy, and the United Kingdom among them, command most of the tourism receipts and international arrivals—the two most common measures of the tourism industry—developing nations have come to rely on tourism as well.

Short History of Tourism

Tourism in Europe dates to ancient Rome. Early tourism was predominantly local and included travel to events like the Roman games. The basics of the tourism industry at the time included inns, taverns, and carriages, many of them regulated by the government. Long-distance travel, which was rare, was accomplished via cargo boats.

During medieval times, the predominant form of tourism was the pilgrimage, with churches and shrines as the main attractions. During the thirteenth and fourteenth centuries, pilgrimages had developed their own tourist infrastructure, including handbooks for travelers and a loose network of hospices.

Over the next two centuries, the religious aims of the pilgrimage were supplanted by desires for pleasure and exposure to new cultures—the two major tourist impulses to this day. Tourists began to travel in search of rare and exotic goods, beautiful scenery, food, sights, and entertainment. Travel came to be considered an important way for young men of the ruling class to learn the ways of the world, thus improving their prospects.

The eighteenth century saw the birth of the "Grand Tour." Young, predominantly aristocratic men traveled through Europe as the final stage of their education, to be steeped in the high culture of France, Italy, and the German states. The Grand Tour thrived until the French Revolution and the Napoleonic Wars inhibited travel. European tourism at this time was the domain of the rich and well educated. As most trips were predicated upon some kind of religious, cultural, or educational agenda, travel sometimes lacked one of the main features of modern tourism—leisure.

Development of Modern Tourism

The evolution of the modern tourism industry has followed developments in the transportation industry—the spread of railways, cars, highways, and civil aviation.

See also:
Globalization;
Transportation Industry.

A promotional poster from 1920 for the St. Moritz Grand Hotel in Switzerland.

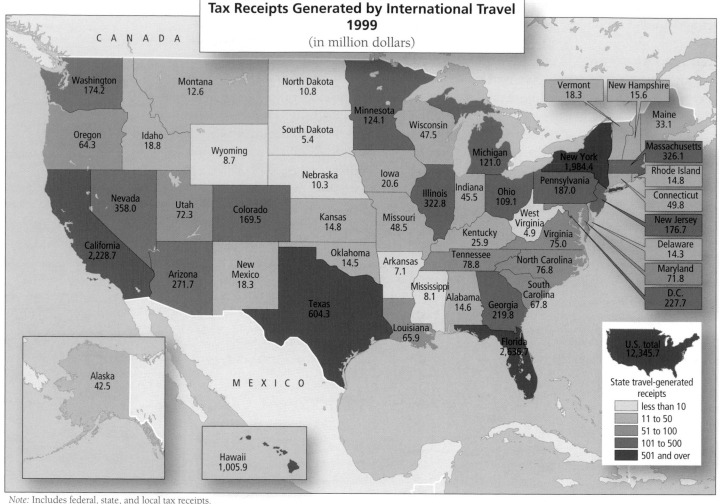

Tax Receipts Generated by International Travel 1999
(in million dollars)

CANADA

Washington 174.2
Montana 12.6
North Dakota 10.8
Minnesota 124.1
Wisconsin 47.5
Michigan 121.0
Vermont 18.3
New Hampshire 15.6
Maine 33.1
Oregon 64.3
Idaho 18.8
South Dakota 5.4
New York 1,984.4
Massachusetts 326.1
Wyoming 8.7
Nebraska 10.3
Iowa 20.6
Illinois 322.8
Indiana 45.5
Ohio 109.1
Pennsylvania 187.0
Rhode Island 14.8
Connecticut 49.8
Nevada 358.0
Utah 72.3
Colorado 169.5
Kansas 14.8
Missouri 48.5
West Virginia 4.9
Virginia 75.0
New Jersey 176.7
Delaware 14.3
California 2,228.7
Kentucky 25.9
Oklahoma 14.5
Arkansas 7.1
Tennessee 78.8
North Carolina 76.8
Maryland 71.8
Arizona 271.7
New Mexico 18.3
Mississippi 8.1
Alabama 14.6
Georgia 219.8
South Carolina 67.8
D.C. 227.7
Texas 604.3
Louisiana 65.9
Florida 2,636.7

MEXICO

Alaska 42.5

Hawaii 1,005.9

U.S. total 12,345.7

State travel-generated receipts
- less than 10
- 11 to 50
- 51 to 100
- 101 to 500
- 501 and over

Note: Includes federal, state, and local tax receipts.

Source: U.S. Bureau of the Census, "Tax Receipts Generated by International Travel," *Statistical Abstracts of the United States,* 2001.

On July 5, 1841, Thomas Cook, who is sometimes called the father of modern mass tourism, organized the first package tour in history, taking 570 passengers on a 20-mile trip by railroad. The rail system, which was nearly complete in Great Britain by the 1840s, made travel for the working classes more feasible. Increased leisure and disposable income—the result of advances in industrialization—helped create more demand for tourism as well. By the 1850s Cook had established himself in a new service industry. Making travel arrangements to destinations as varied as Paris and the Suez Canal, he handled lodging and food as well as language issues, and he created a system of "travelers cheques." Each of Cook's services became a mainstay of the modern travel industry.

The development of automobiles increased tourism, particularly local sightseeing. As automobile touring gained popularity, the United States saw the growth of roadside restaurants, saloons, hotels, and garages. The development of a highway infrastructure by the 1940s was a great boon to automobile touring. Soon, motor lodges, full-service motel chains and restaurants like Howard Johnson's, roadside commercial strips, and car-friendly campgrounds became part of tourism infrastructure in many areas throughout the country.

Gas rationing contributed to a steep decline in recreational travel during World War II, but mass tourism exploded once the war ended. The strong economy and a growing middle class with disposable income and increased leisure were significant contributors to this boom. The Department of Commerce, in one of the earliest statistics related to the tourism industry, declared that in 1949, 62 percent of all Americans took leisure trips. Nearly 80 percent of these trips were made by car or rail; only 4 percent were made by airplane.

Although regular commercial airline service began in the 1920s, airline travel did not become truly accessible to the great majority of people until the 1950s. In 1952 airplanes began to replace railroads and transatlantic ships as the primary mode of long-distance travel. By the mid-1960s international travel had grown so vast that what is now the World Tourism Organization was created to work with organizations like the World Health Organization, UNESCO, and the International Civil Aviation Organization on international tourism. The United Nations General Assembly declared 1967 International Tourist Year.

Niche Tourism

In addition to traditional cultural and leisure tourism, a number of niche markets have evolved.

Ecotourism. By the 1970s, in response to the fledgling environmental movement and growing distaste for prepackaged commercial tours, a movement toward environmentally friendly, culturally sensitive travel began, and the term *ecotourism* bubbled up in the travel lexicon. By the 1990s ecotourism was growing at a rate of 20 percent a year—by far the most swiftly expanding sector of tourism—and governments throughout the world took notice. The United Nations named 2002 the International Year of Ecotourism, and in May 2002 the World Ecotourism Summit convened in Québec.

The International Ecotourism Society defines ecotourism as "responsible travel to

Western tourists visit a model Padaung women's village in north Thailand in 1996.

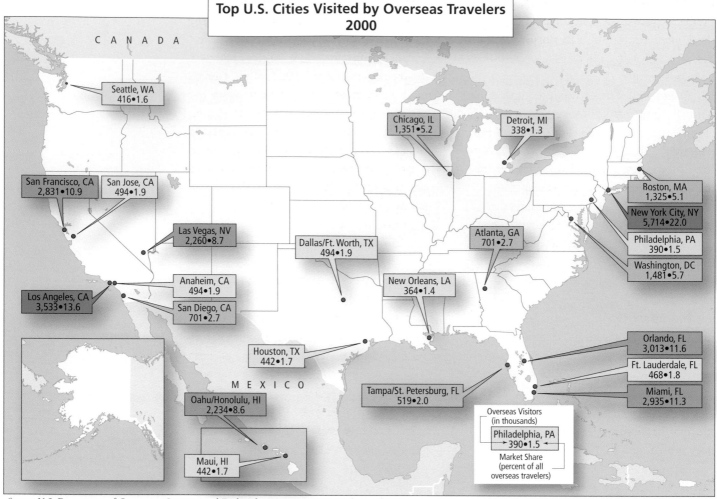

Top U.S. Cities Visited by Overseas Travelers 2000

CANADA

MEXICO

Seattle, WA
416•1.6

Chicago, IL
1,351•5.2

Detroit, MI
338•1.3

Boston, MA
1,325•5.1

New York City, NY
5,714•22.0

Philadelphia, PA
390•1.5

Washington, DC
1,481•5.7

San Francisco, CA
2,831•10.9

San Jose, CA
494•1.9

Las Vegas, NV
2,260•8.7

Dallas/Ft. Worth, TX
494•1.9

Atlanta, GA
701•2.7

Anaheim, CA
494•1.9

New Orleans, LA
364•1.4

Los Angeles, CA
3,533•13.6

San Diego, CA
701•2.7

Houston, TX
442•1.7

Orlando, FL
3,013•11.6

Ft. Lauderdale, FL
468•1.8

Miami, FL
2,935•11.3

Oahu/Honolulu, HI
2,234•8.6

Tampa/St. Petersburg, FL
519•2.0

Maui, HI
442•1.7

Overseas Visitors
(in thousands)

Philadelphia, PA
390•1.5

Market Share
(percent of all
overseas travelers)

Source: U.S. Department of Commerce, International Trade Administration, *Basic Market Analysis Program,* 2001.

natural areas that conserves the environment and sustains the well-being of local people." Ecotourism goes beyond protecting reefs or rain forests or other ecosystems from damage by tourists; it encompasses working with local economies to create sustainable tourism. The ideal ecotourism industries are small in size, staffed by local workers, and stocked with local goods.

However, many companies fall short. In Costa Rica, a renowned ecotourism location, some industries claim to be eco-friendly while offering decidedly nonenvironmentally sound products and practices. Ecotourism certification agencies have sprung up to combat such practices by awarding green labels to companies that meet certain standards.

Health and Medical Tourism. Health care is the world's second largest industry after tourism, and the two industries have long been linked. Throughout time people have traveled for medicinal treatments and alleged cures.

Contemporary health tourism has evolved from mineral baths and spas to include cheap plastic surgery at luxurious private hospitals. Health and medical tourism industries have cropped up in countries like Cuba, India, and Thailand, linking private medical facilities with travel agencies. Servimed, a Cuban medical marketing company, claims that Cuba is the "home of health tourism," lauding its medical advances in the treatment of Parkinson's disease, night blindness, and various skin problems; some of Servimed's treatments are not available in the United States. Tourists from around the world are lured to India's Ayurvedic spas. In Thailand, the Bumrungrad Hospital boasts of cut-rate plastic surgery in deluxe accommodations. Thailand's medical tourism also offers sexual-reassignment surgery, which, in Thailand, costs one-quarter of the price in the United States and is performed without the strict psychological assessments U.S. hospitals require.

Other countries offer package deals, with discount MRIs or complete physicals, along with resort accommodations, where a patient can stroll on the beach while waiting for test results. Medical tourism can also include black-market organ transplants.

Sex Tourism. Sex has long played a role in tourism. For example, seventeenth-century Venice was known throughout Europe for its courtesans. Contemporary sex tourism functions in an ethically gray area. Special, mostly legal, travel agencies and agents arrange flights and accommodations and offer information about the sex industry in another country, where the industry may or may not be legal. Although statistics are impossible to verify, in 1998 *The Economist* estimated that the global sex tourism industry is worth at least $20 billion and probably much more.

The main force behind the recent growth of the sex tourism industry has been the Internet. Some Web sites charge a fee for access to personal accounts of sex tours and worldwide prostitution. As the sex tourism industry has grown from familiar locales, including Cuba, Amsterdam, and Thailand, to countries throughout Southeast Asia, the Caribbean, and beyond, so has awareness of its consequences.

In the 1990s child sex tourism became a global issue. A 1996 conference in Bangkok, End Child Prostitution in Asian Tourism, estimated that one million children in Asia are involved in prostitution. In 1997 the World Tourism Organization founded the Task Force to Protect Children from Sexual Exploitation in Tourism to monitor the problem.

Agritourism. Agritourism is a subset of rural tourism, in which tourists take part in the rural farm economy. Typical examples include visits to dude ranches and working farms. On the local level, agritourism includes fairs and festivals. In Colombia, Fedecafe (National Federation of Coffee Growers) offers tours of coffee plantations as a way to offset economic losses in the volatile coffee market.

Space Tourism. The space tourism industry began in April 2001, when Dennis Tito, an American businessman, ventured into space aboard a Russian rocket. A year later, a South African private citizen made a similar trip. Although Russia has suspended the program because of payment issues (each trip costs $20 million), a handful of businesses worldwide have plans to build the tourist infrastructure for space travel, including orbital hotels and space vehicles.

Contemporary Tourism

According to data released in June 2002, international tourist arrivals in the United States dropped by four million in 2001, from 697 million in 2000, mainly because of fears resulting from the terrorist attacks of September 11, 2001. Attacks on tourist destinations in Bali and Kenya have further disrupted international tourism and prompted the World Tourism Organization to counsel countries on how to limit the negative effect of terrorism on their tourism industries.

The tourist industry is also undergoing changes because of an aging population. A growing number of elderly travelers may lead to a shift in popular destinations, with resort and leisure destinations getting more

Careers in the Tourism Industry

A travel career can be ideal for the individual who enjoys working with people, is flexible, and has good communication skills. The U.S. Bureau of Labor Statistics estimates that in the early years of the twenty-first century, the demand for travel professionals will increase by more than 40 percent.

Although tourism produces jobs, it does not necessarily create high income. Many jobs that are available are unskilled. Average U.S. wages in hospitality, travel, and retailing are anywhere from 5 to 35 percent lower than the national average. A considerable number of jobs are part-time or are temporary because of the seasonal nature of many tourist locations.

Professional career options with a higher level of income and benefits are usually available within travel agencies as leisure and vacation counselors, corporate travel agents, and event planners. Corporations often hire corporate travel arrangers who make travel plans and manage travel budgets. Airlines hire reservationists, flight attendants, and pilots, while hotels maintain a number of professional positions.

—*Theresa Overbey*

Children on Satawal Island, Micronesia, watch a cruise ship anchored off their shore (undated photo).

business than adventure or wilderness trips; locations with mild climates during all four seasons are becoming more popular. Elderly travelers also affect transportation trends, leading to a possible decline in automobile tourism (many elderly do not drive) and an increase in full-service travel packages, with air and ground transportation provided. As the aging baby boom population in the United States nears retirement, the tourism industry expects an increase in vacation and leisure travel.

Technological advances in tourism, for example, online reservation services, can make travel both easier and sometimes less expensive. Although the Internet has adversely affected professional travel agents (who find themselves less necessary than in the past), in general the Internet has been a boon for tourism. However, advances in teleconferencing and other telecommunication technologies may cut business-related travel, especially as

airline ticket prices rise. Successful tourism corporations will have to adjust to these new technologies, embracing more aspects of e-commerce as they strive to remain solvent in the twenty-first century.

Further Reading

Burkart, A. J., and S. Medlik. *Tourism: Past, Present and Future*. 2nd ed. London: Heinemann, 1981.

Feifer, Maxine. *Tourism in History: From Imperial Rome to the Present*. New York: Stein and Day, 1986.

Honey, Martha. *Ecotourism and Sustainable Development: Who Owns Paradise?* Washington, D.C.: Island Press, 1999.

Jakle, John A. *The Tourist: Travel in Twentieth Century North America*. Lincoln: University of Nebraska Press, 1985.

Smith, Valene L., ed. *Hosts and Guests: The Anthropology of Tourism*. Philadelphia: University of Pennsylvania Press, 1977.

—*Laura Lambert*

Trade Associations

Trade associations are voluntary, cooperative organizations formed to provide information about and further the mutual interests of businesses within a particular industry. Closely resembling professional associations and societies, which serve individuals, trade associations serve corporate members. These corporate members are often competitors who nevertheless see value in working together on industry-wide issues.

Found in countries across the world, trade associations represent a full spectrum of producers of goods and services: from machine tools (Association for Manufacturing Technology) to toys (Toy Manufacturers of America), from construction (Association of Equipment Manufacturers) to real estate finance (Mortgage Bankers Association of America). In the United States, trade associations are typically classified under federal law as 501(c)(6), not-for-profit organizations.

Although trade associations vary considerably in focus and size (in the United States the median number of corporate members is approximately 425), typically their objectives include the following:

- Improve and extend the application of products and the specific technologies underlying them.
- Conserve the effort, improve the efficiency, and lower the production cost for the benefit of users as well as providers of the products in question.
- Foster cooperation among users and providers through the development of recommended industry standards and practices.
- Serve as a unified voice in representing the industry to government, other industries, and educators.
- Provide a forum for the industry's study of common problems and objectives.

The idea that representatives of an industry can work together for their mutual benefit is not new. Some evidence is available to show that trade associations may have existed in ancient China and Egypt; they did flourish in Europe as merchant guilds during the fourteenth through sixteenth centuries. Early traders banded together for protection as their caravans traveled across new and often hostile territory. Rules later were developed requiring members of a guild to defend one another in case of legal disputes. As they grew in importance, guilds took on supervisory roles, overseeing training and wholesale and retail trade within a given area.

Today's trade associations still serve protective and surveillance roles, but the means for achieving these ends differ from those of their early counterparts. Many associations now monitor government policies (trade pacts, tariffs, environmental regulations, and labor laws, for example) that might affect their members' businesses. Associations may strive to influence such policies through lobbying; they may organize campaigns among their members, recruiting them to contact lawmakers in efforts to affect the outcome of pending legislation. Some participate in PACs (political action committees) supporting the campaigns of candidates for office believed to support their particular interests.

Trade associations no longer directly supervise how products are bought and sold, but many certainly monitor the processes. For example, many associations track their industry's shipments and orders, and the resulting reports are widely viewed as industry barometers. Associations collect other statistical and market data on

See also:
Chambers of Commerce;
ISO 9000; Price Fixing;
Professional Associations.

Some Activities of Trade Associations

- Monitor products
- Collect statistical and marketing data
- Develop industry-wide standards
- Educate members
- Monitor government policies
- Lobby government officials

Challenges and Opportunities in the Twenty-first Century	
Challenges	**Opportunities**
• Business consolidation reduces association membership pool • Downsizing and recession decrease amounts association members can afford to dedicate • Once-proprietary industry information now readily available over Internet	• Internet links members worldwide • Web forums facilitate standards development • Web-conferencing facilitates distance-learning programs • Virtual trade shows expedite information

behalf of their members, and they often provide or track economic forecasts. Trade associations must avoid any activity that could be construed as price fixing, which is prohibited by law.

Associations play an active role in the development of industry-wide standards (for the manufacture of lightbulbs or hydraulic valves, for example). Standards are developed to ensure that products will deliver an expected level of performance and that they will work compatibly and safely in larger systems. Some standards also define the symbols and terminology to facilitate communication among designers, manufacturers, and users. For example, in a hydraulic fluid power system, power is transmitted and controlled through a liquid under pressure within an enclosed circuit. The safe and efficient application of components within a hydraulic system requires precise communication between the manufacturer and the user of the components; such communication is facilitated by industry-wide acceptance of published standards. Industry standards are developed by volunteer committees working through associations. Their work is increasingly international in scope (the ISO 9000 standards are one example), requiring the cooperative effort of company representatives and associations around the globe.

Education is another cornerstone of association activity. Trade associations provide education for their industries by sponsoring seminars, workshops, and technical conferences for members. They also inform outside audiences about the industries they represent through expositions, promotional campaigns in the trade press, and through Internet sites.

Associations always have faced a need to adapt to changing circumstances. That need appears more pressing than ever early in the twenty-first century. Business consolidation in many industries has reduced the association membership pool; hence the cost of member services is necessarily divided among fewer companies. Time and ready hands also seem to be increasingly scarce. Associations rely on volunteers. Downsizing and recession in some industries have decreased the amount of effort association members can afford to dedicate to developing standards, contributing to statistical surveys, and participating in industry seminars and conferences—all mainstays of association services.

New technologies also create threats. Although some industry-relevant information is still proprietary to association members, other data once provided through association channels are now readily available on the Internet. For-profit companies, particularly those seeking to serve as industry-specific Web portals (Web sites that offer many resources—forums, search engines, product malls, and so on), are challenging the traditional roles of trade associations by offering similar services.

At the same time, new technology can also be used to develop improved and extended association services. Some associations use Web forums to facilitate standards development. Web-enabled conferencing makes possible the development of distance learning programs—members now can participate in many association programs without leaving their desks. Software programs enable members to make better use of the statistical data that associations provide. Internet sites, with multiple links to sites worldwide, together with virtual trade shows, expedite information exchange of the sort that has always been a principal value of trade association membership.

Trade associations have thrived over centuries because their members believe they can do more together than any one of them might accomplish individually. The problems to be solved continue to change, but a belief in the power of association continues.

Further Reading

Downs, Buck, ed. *Directory of National Trade and Professional Associations of the United States 2002*. Washington, D.C.: Columbia Books, 2002.

———. *National Trade and Professional Association*. Washington, D.C.: Columbia Books, 2001.

Paull, Irving S., J. W. Millard, and James S. Taylor. *Trade Association Activities*. Buffalo, N.Y.: W. S. Hein, 1983.

Williams, Steven. "Pace-Setting Practices." *Association Management*, November 2001, 49–56.

World Guide to Trade Associations: Chambers of Industry and Commerce. 6th ed. Munich, Germany: K. G. Saur, 2003.

—Linda Western

Trade associations sometimes involve themselves in politics. In 2002 the Hawaii Technology and Trade Association and the Hawaii Venture Capital Association cosponsored a forum in which gubernatorial candidates Mazie Hirono, left, and Linda Lingle, right, answered questions about technology issues.

See also:
Copyright; Intellectual Property; License; Patent.

Trademark

Trademarks are the images, words, signs, and symbols that corporations use to represent the products and services they offer. Trademarks began with the brands, marks, and tattoos that identified the livestock of a farm or ranch. Such marks of identity, ownership, and origin go back more than five millennia to the great empires of the Middle East. Royal marks, heraldry, and monograms identified the owners of public and private property and certified the origin of products.

As trade grew in the Mediterranean region and beyond, these marks came to include the marks found on ancient ceramic artifacts. The first true trademarks were in use by the time of the Roman Empire, where they identified the oil lamps manufactured by such early multinational firms as Fortis and Stroboli. In time, watermarks, quarry gang marks, mason guild marks, hallmarks, assay marks, and furniture marks all came to serve the twin functions that trademarks serve today.

The Role of Trademarks

The first function is to inform the public that a specific organization or individual makes a product or provides a service. Public law protects trademark rights as a form of intellectual property. Trademark law enables those who invest in providing goods and services to protect their investment by securing the sole right to be identified with their own products and services. This encourages enterprise, increases the flow of investment, and increases the opportunities for profit.

The second function of trademarks is to signal the attributes and level of quality that can be expected of the product or service offered. It constitutes a form of public information and helps to regulate markets. By permitting trademarks to function as quality guarantees, this aspect of the law increases the transparency of markets. In this way, the law helps to secure the rights of investors, firms, and consumers.

A trademark is an information artifact. As a tag or marker, it has no true value apart from its connection to a good or service. The good or service could exist without the trademark, but the trademark would not have the same meaning without the good or service with which it is associated. Nevertheless, the value of a trademark is so closely connected to the good or service it represents that many trademarks take on a special value of their own.

Repeated and consistent use of a respected trademark endows it with the significance of the underlying products and services that the trademark represents. Customers who prefer a product or service

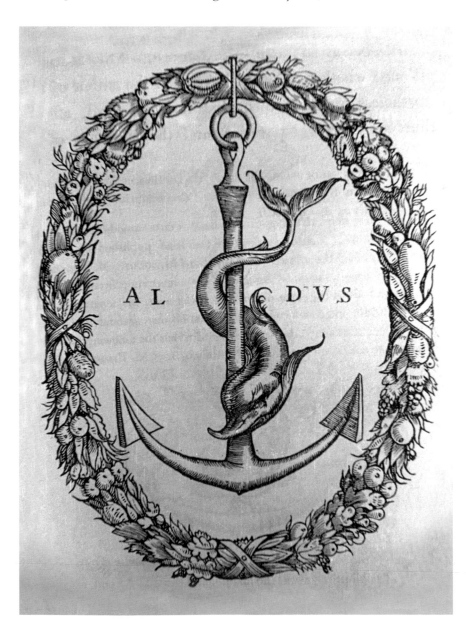

A fifteenth-century trademark belonging to Aldus Manutius, a Venetian printer.

Trademarks 1980 to 2001 (in thousands)									
	1980	1985	1990	1995	1997	1998	1999	2000	2001
Applications filed	46.8	65.1	127.3	188.9	234.6	246.6	328.6	296.5	232.9
Trademarks issued	24.7	71.7	60.8	92.5	145.2	136.1	191.9	115.2	133.8

Source: U.S. Patent and Trademark Office, "Statistical Reports Available for Viewing Calendar Year Patent Statistics," http://www.uspto.gov/web/offices/ac/ido/oeip/taf/reports.htm (April 5, 2003).

seek it out, creating market value for the provider. This market value is called brand equity. Brand equity and the value of a trademark constitute part of the intellectual capital of an organization.

In some circumstances, the significance of a trademark can take on value in its own right. The organization that owns a trademark can legitimately use it to extend meaning and guarantee the quality of other related products and services. Used illegally, the trademark can be attached to products or services from other providers. This activity—known as piracy or counterfeiting—allows those who have not invested in the development of a trademark to take the profits that the trademark represents, usually at a lower cost than the costs of the true trademark owner.

For individual firms and organizations, counterfeiting represents an immediate cost, a loss of business, and a threat to markets. This form of piracy once mostly concerned specific firms or trademark owners. The international flow of goods and services is now so great that it has become an issue of international concern. Trade flows in trademarked goods and services constitute a massive part of the global economy. These flows affect huge portions of the trade balance of every industrial nation. Accordingly, trademark law is now a matter of international treaty.

Organizations of all kinds use trademarks. Manufacturers and service firms, public agencies, governments, and nonprofit organizations use them along with universities, professional associations, and churches. Trademarks identify tangible

products and immaterial services. They help consumers to recognize the information products and virtual services of the knowledge economy.

Further Reading

Aaker, David A. *Managing Brand Equity: Capitalizing on the Value of a Brand Name.* Collingdale, Pa.: DIANE Publishing, 2000.

Cristal, Lisa E., and Neals S. Greenfield, eds. *Trademark Law and the Internet: Issues, Case Law, and Practice Tips.* New York: International Trademark Association, 2002.

Fletcher, Anthony L., and David J. Kera, eds. *2000 Trademark Handbook U.S. and International.* Vol. 1. New York: International Trademark Association, 2000.

Legal Information Institute. "Trademark Law: An Overview." http://www.law.cornell.edu/topics/trademark.html (March 27, 2003).

Olins, Wally. *Corporate Identity: Making Business Strategy Visible through Design.* Boston: Harvard Business School Press, 1990.

Shilling, Dana. *Essentials of Trademarks and Unfair Competition.* New York: John Wiley & Sons, 2002.

—*Ken Friedman*

Trademark Symbols		
Mark	Definition	Use
TM	A word, name, symbol or device that is used in trade with goods to indicate the source of the goods and to distinguish them from the goods of others	Alerts public of claim of rights in a mark
SM	Same as a trademark except that it identifies and distinguishes the source of a service (banking, dry cleaning, transportation, house painting, etc.)	
®	Registered trademark	May be used only after the U.S. Patent and Trademark Office registers the mark

Source: U.S. Patent and Trademark Office, "What Are Patents, Trademarks, Servicemarks, and Copyrights?" http://www.uspto.gov/web/offices/pac/doc/general/whatis.htm (March 18, 2003).

Trade Policy

Trade policy refers to various government policies used to influence the flow of goods and services across a country's borders. The purpose of these policies is to create a trade environment that represents the most favorable business conditions that can coexist with the government's economic growth philosophy and the attitudes of the nation toward international trade. Different kinds of trade polices have different effects on specific sectors of the domestic economy and on the country in general.

Import-Limiting Policies

Trade policies that are designed to reduce imports—the flow of goods or services produced in other countries—are import-limiting policies. For example, tariffs (taxes imposed on imports) are predominantly used as part of an import-limiting strategy—although in some developing counties the primary purpose of some tariffs is to generate government revenues.

Nontariff barriers to imports include import quotas, voluntary export restraints (VERs), product standards, and domestic content requirements. Import quotas are a domestic government mandate limiting the amount of a particular good allowed to be imported from another country.

The VER is similar to a quota. The importing country convinces the foreign producer's country to "voluntarily" limit the amount of goods that it exports. In persuading the foreign country to enact a VER, the importing country becomes worse off in general because it forgoes all

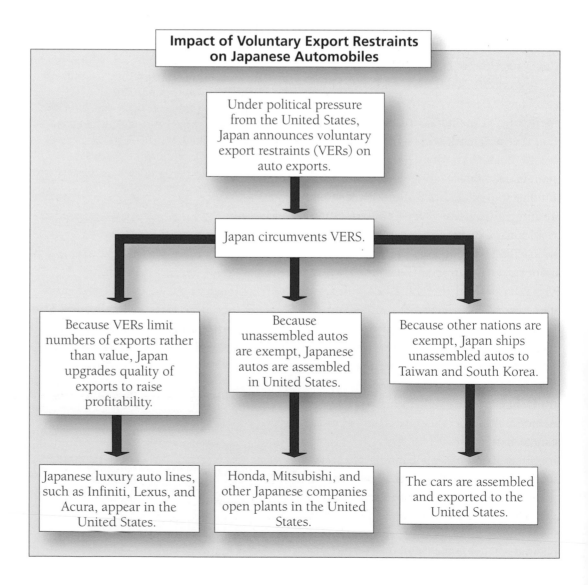

Impact of Voluntary Export Restraints on Japanese Automobiles

Under political pressure from the United States, Japan announces voluntary export restraints (VERs) on auto exports.

Japan circumvents VERS.

Because VERs limit numbers of exports rather than value, Japan upgrades quality of exports to raise profitability.

Because unassembled autos are exempt, Japanese autos are assembled in United States.

Because other nations are exempt, Japan ships unassembled autos to Taiwan and South Korea.

Japanese luxury auto lines, such as Infiniti, Lexus, and Acura, appear in the United States.

Honda, Mitsubishi, and other Japanese companies open plants in the United States.

The cars are assembled and exported to the United States.

the revenues that would have been gained if it enacted a tariff instead of a VER. VERs are frequently used as a political solution to address a desire to continue free trade policies yet also supply some temporary support for certain sectors of the economy. For example, in the 1980s the United States used VERs to help the auto industry reorganize while attempting to maintain market share under what was believed to be short-term competitive pressures from Japanese automakers.

Other forms of import restriction include the imposition of excessive product standards to raise the cost of producing the imported goods and the banning of certain production methods—and therefore the companies that use those production methods. The beef dispute between the United States and the European Union (E.U.) is an example. The United States uses various

growth hormones in the raising of cattle; the European Union contends that human health is threatened by the use of these hormones. The scientific evidence to support this position is disputed. The European Union's use of product standards effectively reduces the amount of U.S. beef imported into the European Union and thus acts as a protectionist measure aiding the E.U. cattle industry. The 1999–2001 crisis involving

Japanese vehicles at a used car lot in Yokohama, Japan, in 2001. Especially in the 1980s, the United States placed trade restrictions on Japanese car imports to protect its domestic industries.

Types of Trade Policy

Import-Limiting Policies	Policies for Pushing Exports
• Tariffs	• Dumping goods
• Import quotas	• Government subsidies
• VERs (voluntary export restraints)	
• Product standards	
• Domestic content requirements	

mad cow disease (bovine spongiform encephalopathy) in Europe served only to intensify the beef controversy, as the United States began rejecting beef from Europe, and European countries argued among themselves about their beef imports.

Arguments for Protection

Many economically sound arguments can be advanced for protection when some domestic or international market failure exists for a particular economic sector or individual good. For example, when some form of pricing distortion is in place because of monopoly power (the ability of the seller to adjust price), monopsony power (the ability of the buyer to adjust market price), externalities in production (additional costs to economy not included in the production costs), or externalities in consumption (additional benefits to the economy not included in the market price), then the implementation of a trade policy to correct the market failure may make economic sense. Economists generally see using trade policy to correct market failures as acceptable when the trade policy's benefits outweigh the costs to the economy.

One of the more widely used protectionist arguments is the infant industry argument, which maintains that protection of the domestic industry from foreign competition is warranted during the establishment and initial stages of a domestic industry. The infant industry argument contends that the domestic industry needs a chance to obtain the skills and economies of scale to compete with the more developed foreign industry. Such support could be accomplished by a direct subsidy (a payment to

A butcher stands behind a piece of British beef at the meat counter of Sainsburys supermarket during an October 1999 promotion of British meat products in London.

the producers or consumers by a third party, normally the government, to reduce the price of a good) or previously discussed trade policies. Other protectionist arguments involve the pursuit of noneconomic objects, including a national desire to be self-sufficient or an ability to maintain a critical domestic industry that produces certain national defense goods.

Free and Fair Trade

Some of the most-watched trade policy practices occur in countries that have directly or indirectly condoned business practices to increase exports through anti-competitive means. For example, dumping is the practice of selling exports at a price lower than the price at home or lower than the average cost of production. Exporters may engage in dumping to drive down prices and remove rivals; this is considered to be predatory activity and is not condoned as a fair trade practice. Importing countries generally watch for dumping by exporting countries and take measures to stop the practice by retaliating with their own trade restrictions or negotiating for a favorable compromise with the dumping nation. Some of the most cited complaints to the World Trade Organization are allegations that a country is creating an unfair trade atmosphere by subsidizing a particular industry—paying export producers money to reduce production costs.

Each country implements trade policies according to its own interests and philosophies about free trade and protectionism. Throughout the world, the general trend seems to be in a direction of freer trade. International trade agreements have been emerging to create areas that offer the signatory countries access to each other's markets unimpeded by protectionist trade policies. These agreements include free trade zones like the North American Free Trade Area among Canada, Mexico, and the United States.

An accord with even greater social and economic integration is the European Union, which in 2003 included 15 European

Foreign Exchange Losses as a Result of U.S. Cotton Subsidies in Selected Countries 2001 to 2002 (in million dollars)	
Country	Value Lost as a Result of U.S. Subsidies
Benin	33
Burkina Faso	28
Cameroon	21
Chad	16
Cote d'Ivoire	32
Mali	43
Nigeria	14
Sudan	17
Tanzania	21
Togo	16
Zimbabwe	18

Source: Oxfam, "Cultivating Poverty: The Impact of U.S. Cotton Subsidies on Africa," Oxfam Briefing Paper 30, http://www.oxfam.org/eng/pdfs/pp020925_cotton.pdf (March 18, 2003).

nations that had extended their integration past free trade polices to include many other interactions between their countries. Twelve additional nations, many from the former Soviet bloc, were scheduled to become a part of the European Union in 2004; other applications, that of Turkey for one, were also under review. The World Trade Organization represents another structure that oversees various trade agreements for over 130 member nations whose general trend is toward open, free international markets. This trend toward free international trade and globalization of industry is expected to continue well into the future.

Government subsidies can be good for domestic producers but bad for international trade. For example, most African nations cannot compete against heavily subsidized U.S. cotton.

Further Reading

Bhagwati, Jagdish N. *The Feuds over Free Trade.* Singapore: Institute of Southeast Asian Studies, 1997.

Burniaux, Jean-Marc. *Trade Policies in a Global Context.* Paris: Organization for Economic Co-operation and Development, 1991.

Carbaugh, Robert J. *International Economics.* 8th ed. Cincinnati, Ohio: South-Western Publishing, 2001.

Caves, Richard E., Jeffrey A. Frankel, and Ronald W. Jones. *World Trade and Payments: An Introduction.* 9th ed. Reading, Mass.: Addison Wesley, 2002.

Gerber, James. *International Economics.* 2nd ed. Boston: Addison-Wesley, 2002.

—James K. Self

Tragedy of the Commons

The concept known as tragedy of the commons explains the overuse of resources held in common—resources that are not privately owned. It is a useful concept for understanding environmental problems, including excessive fishing and the overuse of grazing land.

The term itself was coined by biologist Garrett Hardin in a 1968 *Science* magazine article. Perhaps because Hardin's article was written as the modern environmental movement was getting underway, it touched a nerve and quickly became well known. "This is probably one of the most cited articles among social scientists in this period, and it is surely the most reprinted," writes Michael Taylor, a political scientist at the University of Washington.

In the article Hardin described a commonly owned pasture. Traditionally, in England such pastures developed near a village. They provided good grazing land for livestock as long as the village was small and only a few people grazed their animals on the common. However, as more villagers used a pasture, it would become overcrowded and overgrazed, so that grass could not grow back in the following year.

Excessive use of the pasture ultimately hurt all the villagers. No one sought such an outcome, Hardin explained; instead, overuse occurred because of common ownership. Each villager had an incentive to graze another cow on the pasture even after the pasture's carrying capacity had been reached. The villager who added a cow received the full benefit for doing so—a cow nourished by all the grass it could eat—but this villager did not pay the full cost of depleting the grass. The cost of overgrazing was shared among all the villagers. With pastures open to all, this difference between the personal cost to individual villagers (low) and the social cost to communities (high) led to too much grazing.

Of course a villager might foresee the potential harm and might wish to limit grazing. With common ownership, however, the villager would have no right to tell others what to do—all were equal. As long as one person wanted to exploit the common, others could not protect it. As the costs involved were shared while the benefits were individually enjoyed, each villager had an incentive to take action that could be costly to the group. Common ownership created perverse incentives.

Tragedy of the Commons

Each herder keeps as many cattle as possible in a common pasture.

⬇

Tribal wars, poaching, and disease keep the numbers of people and cattle below carrying capacity of the common.

⬇

Social stability achieved.

⬇

Each herder is compelled to add another animal to his herd to maximize individual gain.

⬇

Herd exceeds capacity of common.

⬇

Common becomes overgrazed; cattle stunted.

Hong Kong's crowded Aberdeen Harbor in 1999.

The tragedy of the commons analysis helps to explain what happens to many natural resources. It explains why some species of whales are pushed to the brink of extinction. Each whaler has an incentive to take a whale from the ocean. The whaler receives the full benefit of capturing the whale but pays little of the cost. Even if some whalers foresee a pending disaster, they cannot force others to hold back. The "rule of capture" prevails— the person who gets the whale first reaps benefits at the expense of others, including other whalers.

The tragedy of the commons concept has been reanalyzed over the years. Some commentators stress that common ownership may not pose a problem if access to the resource is restricted. For example, a coastal fishing village that keeps outsiders from

> Ruin is the destination toward which all men rush, each pursuing his own best interest in a society that believes in the freedom of the commons. Freedom in a commons brings ruin to all.
>
> —Garrett Hardin, "The Tragedy of the Commons," 1968

fishing in the estuary would be less likely to experience the tragedy. Traditional customs and rules like stinting (limiting the number of animals per villager) can turn a common into what Hardin called a managed common. The concept has also been expanded to describe cases of air and water pollution. Air and water, in most cases, are "commons"—nobody owns them. A polluting factory may exploit these commons by discharging soot and chemicals into them.

What is to be done about commons? In "The Tragedy of the Commons" and a later essay, Hardin identified three possibilities: private ownership, government regulation, and traditional customs.

Although Hardin did not endorse private property rights as the preferred solution, his framing of the issue highlighted the potential benefits of private ownership. Had the pasture been privately owned, a villager would have benefited from grazing cows on it, but he or she also would have had to pay all costs arising from grazing too many animals there. The villager would be positioned to receive benefits and to pay costs; this pattern of incentives would encourage limits on grazing. Furthermore, the owner would have the right and the incentive to keep others from grazing cattle on the land.

An alternative to private ownership is government regulation. Such regulation of commonly held air and water is generally not controversial, but government regulation of other commons, fisheries, for example, has produced spotty results and heightened interest in alternative approaches. A 1999 report by the U.S. National Marine Fisheries Service found, for example, that 98 species currently being fished in U.S. territorial waters are being overfished despite extensive regulation. This represents 42.6 percent of the fish species studied by the service. Other species among the 674 species not studied to date are also probably being overfished. The government's failure to control overfishing has spurred an interest in individually tradable quotas for fishing. The commons problem is addressed by giving each fisher the right to a specified portion of the total catch. Fishers can trade these quotas, getting in and out of the business as they wish. Such quotas are an attempt to bring a measure of private ownership to fisheries commons.

The idea that commonly owned property is poorly treated is not new. It goes back at least as far as Aristotle. He wrote in *Politics* that "what is common to many is taken least care of, for all men have greater regard for what is their own than for what they possess in common with others." Long after Aristotle, Hardin tells us, William Forster Lloyd, a political economist, observed in 1832 that the commonly owned pastures in England had "puny and stunted" cattle. "Why is the common itself so bare-worn, and cropped so differently from the adjoining inclosures?" Lloyd asked.

Thanks to Hardin, a concept long understood received new attention. It continues to arouse intense interest and foster discussion as people work at the first step required for solving environmental problems—understanding their causes.

Further Reading

Cesar, Herman S. J. *Control and Game Models of the Greenhouse Effect: Economic Essays on the Comedy and Tragedy of the Commons.* New York: Springer-Verlag, 1994.

Hardin, Garrett. "The Tragedy of the Commons." *Science* (1968): 1243–1248.

Leal, Donald R. *Homesteading the Oceans: The Case for Property Rights in U.S. Fisheries.* PERC Policy Series PS-19. Bozeman, Mont.: Political Economy Research Center, 2000.

Soden, Dennis L. *The Tragedy of the Commons: Twenty Years of Policy Literature, 1968–1988.* Monticello, Ill.: Vance Bibliographies, 1989.

Taylor, Michael. "The Economics and Politics of Property Rights and Common Pool Resources," *Natural Resources Journal* 32 (Summer 1992): 633–648.

—*Jane S. Shaw*

Transportation Industry

From its inception the transportation industry has shaped modern civilization by moving goods and services throughout the world. It remains one of the largest and most influential industries in the United States; in 2000 the U.S. transportation industry taken as a whole constituted 10.7 percent of the nation's entire gross domestic product. That year Americans spent more than $800 billion on private transportation, including auto parts and gasoline; they spent more than $40 billion on local for-hire transportation (buses, trains, and taxis), more than $71 billion on train, bus, and air transportation between cities, and almost $20 billion on international transportation. The transportation industry can be divided into four major categories: shipping, railroads, automobiles, and aviation.

Shipping

Shipping, the act of moving goods and people across water, is perhaps the oldest form of transportation. Prehistoric civilizations were settled near major waterways to allow inhabitants to take advantage of water as a way to get from one place to another. Ancient Egyptians, Greeks, and Romans all relied on major waterways. Not only did they build their own ships for transportation, they also developed small shipping organizations to facilitate the organized exchange of their wares.

Explorers like Christopher Columbus also used ships to reach uncharted parts of the world. Commercial shipping developed significantly in the thirteenth century in Spain and Portugal. The industry soon spread to the rest of Europe. Ships were used for fishing, exploring, and coordinating the exchange of goods and services.

Innovations in shipping technology, for example, the development of the steam engine, improved the shipping industry in modern times. The role of shipping in many international conflicts also cannot be ignored, as troops and weapons often travel on ships. The strength of the U.S. shipping industry has ebbed and flowed over the years, often based on a need for ships during wartime. For example, the U.S. fleet played a critical role in World War II when an assembly line system was used to expedite the construction of ships.

Most people now use faster forms of transportation to get to their destination. However, the American shipping industry still plays a pivotal role in exporting and importing.

Railroads

The railroad is another mode of transport that was more widely used before the rise of automobiles and airplanes, but the railroad industry remains an important component of the transportation industry as a whole. The earliest mention of a railway can be found in Georgius Agricola's book *De re metallica* in 1556, which talks about a railway running on wooden poles. Those poles were replaced by iron rails in the eighteenth century.

Richard Trevithick built the first locomotive in 1804. The first steam-powered system for moving cargo and people started in England in the 1820s. France followed with a rail system a few years later and

See also:
FedEx; Ford, Henry; General Motors; Infrastructure; Southwest Airlines; Tourism Industry.

A print by Currier and Ives of a railway junction in 1876.

other systems sprouted all over Europe in the middle of the nineteenth century.

In the United States, the first railway that used horse-drawn carts was built in the mid-1820s in Massachusetts to carry minerals. Americans started building their own railway cars at that time. The Baltimore & Ohio Railroad opened in 1828, using horse-drawn cars. Steam power came on the scene in the 1830s. Most short rail lines were initially constructed on the East Coast; not until the 1850s did railroads connect to parts of the Midwest, including Chicago. The first transcontinental railroad project was completed in 1869 when the Union Pacific Railroad was connected to the Central Pacific. It ran across the continent from the East Coast to California and took several years to build.

During the Civil War, both sides used the railroads extensively to transport troops and goods. During this rapid expansion many leaders of the industry abused power. The Interstate Commerce Commission (ICC) was created to regulate the industry in 1887. After World War I, the railroad industry boom began to wane, mostly because of widespread use of the automobile.

In 1970 the Rail Passenger Service Act created a National Railroad Passenger Corporation to operate passenger service between most major cities. The operation, Amtrak, now maintains and uses more than 20,000 miles of track in the United States. City dwellers and those in the suburbs rely on trains every day to commute to their jobs. Transportation of commercial freight also remains a major national operation. In 1996 the top 10 railroad companies had revenues of nearly $33 billion.

Automobiles

Railroads would no doubt have an even larger influence on daily life had the automobile, which dates to the late eighteenth century, not been invented. The first self-propelled vehicle appeared in France in 1789. Richard Trevithick, who also built the first locomotive, produced a steam-driven car in 1801. At that point, the vehicles could not go very fast. The internal combustion engine was invented in the 1800s, inspiring a series of new car models in Germany. In the late 1800s the famous Stanley brothers from Massachusetts began to produce steam-driven cars, Stanley Steamers, that were popular until after World War I.

After the war the automobile industry blossomed. The automobile was considered a luxury for most people at that time, but the growth of the road system and eventually the highway system, combined with the more affordable cars produced by the Ford Motor Company, changed America's outlook on cars. Initially cars were rather standard in design, but advances in technology and a greater understanding of aerodynamics led the industry to try several different models. Cars are now often made on an assembly line where tasks are automated to ensure quality and safety.

Americans rely on cars to get nearly everywhere, and many families have more than one automobile. Consumers choose

Commuters waiting for a train from Bethesda, Maryland, into Washington, D.C.

from cars, sport utility vehicles, and trucks when picking a personal vehicle and can choose buses or even limousines to get around on the roads with another driver at the helm. Many cars are made in the United States, but customers also choose models from Japan, Korea, Germany, and Sweden. Not only does the automobile industry play a major role in the economy, but the support industries, for example, auto repair, also employ thousands of people nationwide. Companies that rely on auto transportation to ship their products also employ trained automobile technicians and specialists.

Aviation

The aviation industry is the most recent component of the transportation industry, but it does have an extensive history. The most famous pilots in U.S. history are Orville and Wilbur Wright, who hit the skies off a beach in North Carolina in 1903. However, documented interest in aviation and early discoveries dates to Leonardo da Vinci, who created designs for early planes. In the nineteenth century, several English and French inventors started work on designs that mirror the modern airplane. W. S. Henson of England first patented a design very similar to an airplane in 1842. John Stringfellow built the model plane that became the first

Nissan imports in Seattle, Washington, in 1993.

Careers in the Transportation Industry

The transportation field employs millions of people across the globe in a variety of capacities that generally require training but might not require extensive education after high school. In most states those who wish to drive a car, bus, or truck for a living must pass a special driver's license test. Many attend special driving courses to be more prepared for the work of professional driving, and some private trucking companies require special certification before they will hire an individual.

Train conductors generally receive their training on the job and might begin by taking tickets or assisting the conductor before assuming full responsibility. Pilots and ship captains require more training and often go through flight or aeronautical school to earn certification to operate either mode of transportation. In the United States, many receive such training in the military.

The transportation industry also employs people who are trained to repair the different modes of transportation. Most people receive training at either a technical school or in an apprenticeship program before becoming an auto mechanic. For planes, trains, and ships, more advanced training or schooling is usually required because of increased safety concerns with those forms of transit. The field also has many managerial positions and hires people to assemble the different forms of transit. Most planes, automobiles, ships, and trains are put together on an assembly line.

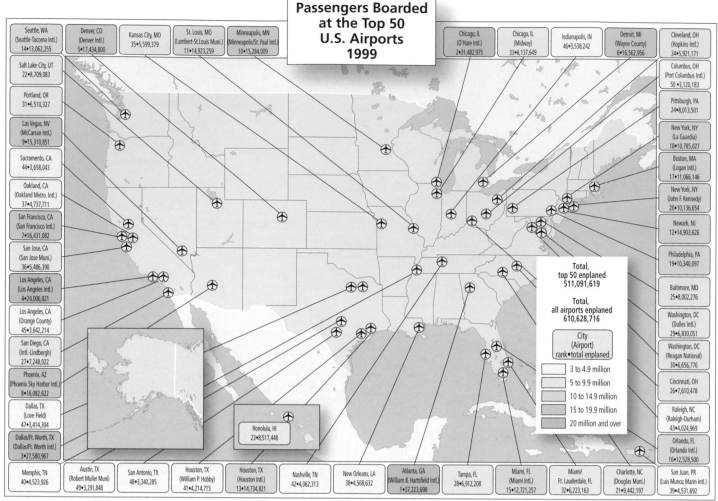

Passengers Boarded at the Top 50 U.S. Airports 1999

Note: Rank order determined by total enplaned passengers on large certificated U.S. air carriers, scheduled and nonscheduled operations, at all airports served within the 50 states, the District of Columbia, and other U.S. areas. Large certificated air carriers operate aircraft with seating capacity of more than 60 seats or a payload capacity of more than 18,000 pounds. Data for commuter, intrastate, and foreign-flag air carriers are not included.
Source: U.S. Bureau of Transportation Statistics, Office of Airline Information, *Airport Activity Statistics,* 2000.

power-driven machine to fly during that era. Hiram Maxim built a plane in England that carried three men into the air via a steam-powered track in 1884.

After World War II, commercial air service came into its own when jet propulsion, radar, and other inventions spurred the process. National guidelines to ensure safety are very strict for airplane construction, which is largely dominated in the United States by Boeing Company. Although statistics show a person is more likely to die in a car crash, plane crashes have taken the lives of thousands of Americans since the industry began, and the industry is closely watched by regulators, including the Federal Aviation Administration.

Airplanes play a major role in the American transportation industry, serving millions of customers each year for both pleasure and business. The industry is fiercely competitive, especially between urban centers. Most air travel is made on fewer than a dozen major carriers, but smaller carriers service less utilized routes. The airline industry has also allowed for overnight shipping and faster mail service.

Further Reading

Fradkin, Phillip. *Stagecoach: Wells Fargo and the American West.* New York: Simon & Schuster, 2002.

Miller, Al. *Tin Stackers: The History of the Pittsburgh Steamship Company.* Detroit, Mich.: Wayne State University Press, 1999.

Wolf, Winifred. *CarMania: A Critical History of Transport, 1770–1990.* London: Pluto Press, 1996.

—*Karen Ayres*

Trippe, Juan

1899–1981
Commercial aviation pioneer

Aviator Juan Trippe did not invent the jet engine or the jet aircraft. Nevertheless, he did more than anyone else to usher in the jet age and make long-distance travel affordable for almost everyone.

A Passion for Flight
Trippe first became interested in flying when he was 10 years old and his father took him to see an air race between the Wright Brothers and Glenn Curtiss. In 1917, as an undergraduate student at Yale, Trippe took classes at the Curtiss Flying School. Trippe left Yale that same year to enlist in the navy and fight in World War I. Trippe trained as a navy bomber pilot, but he never saw action, and returned to Yale at the end of the war.

After graduating in 1921, Trippe spent two years as a bond salesman on Wall Street, but his true passion lay in aviation. He used an inheritance to start an air taxi service—Long Island Airways. When that venture failed in 1924, he raised money from his wealthy Yale friends and formed Eastern Air Transport.

Trippe and some friends were able to convince Congressman M. Clyde Kelly (R–Pennsylvania) of the potential benefits of having some U.S. mail carried by private airlines. This led to the 1925 Kelly Act, which provided mail subsidies to private airlines for delivering U.S. mail. To exploit this opportunity, Trippe helped create Colonial Air Transport; he succeeded in getting a contract for Colonial to deliver mail from Boston to New York via Hartford.

During a publicity flight to Cuba to show off Colonial's new Fokker trimotor airplane, Trippe obtained an appointment with Cuban president Gerardo Machado. (Although Trippe was not Hispanic—he was named after a favorite aunt, Juanita—he often found it easier to conduct business if people assumed he was of Spanish extraction). During their meeting, President Machado agreed to give Trippe exclusive rights to land at Camp Colombia, Havana's army airport. Trippe resigned from Colonial in 1927, taking the Cuban landing agreement with him.

The Golden Age of the Flying Boats
Trippe now formed yet another airline, Aviation Corporation of America, with two coworkers from Colonial. To finance the route to Cuba, the airline almost immediately merged with two others to form Pan American Airways, with Trippe as president and general manager.

Trippe and Pan Am now began to pioneer new routes, and in 1934 Trippe announced that Pan Am would begin service across the Pacific. At the time such

See also:
Competition; Price Fixing; Tourism Industry; Transportation Industry.

Juan Trippe in an undated portrait.

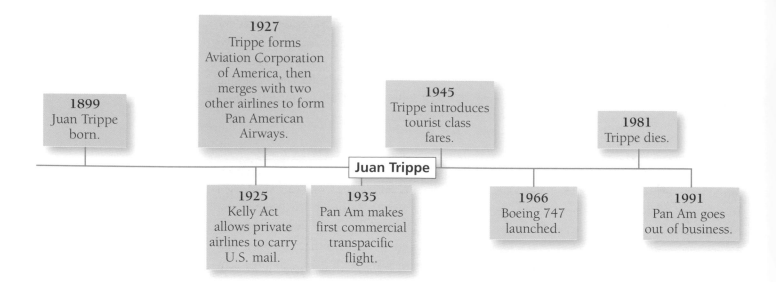

1899
Juan Trippe born.

1927
Trippe forms Aviation Corporation of America, then merges with two other airlines to form Pan American Airways.

1945
Trippe introduces tourist class fares.

1981
Trippe dies.

Juan Trippe

1925
Kelly Act allows private airlines to carry U.S. mail.

1935
Pan Am makes first commercial transpacific flight.

1966
Boeing 747 launched.

1991
Pan Am goes out of business.

flights were thought to be impossible—aviators argued that refueling stops were too few in the Pacific between the United States and China. Undeterred, Trippe purchased several Martin M-130s, the first of the great China Clipper flying boats. Powered by four Pratt & Whitney Wasp engines, these planes had a range of 3,200 miles and could land in the water, eliminating the need for expensive concrete runways. The first commercial transpacific flight left California on November 23, 1935. Five days later it arrived in Manila, via Midway, Wake, and Guam.

Pan Am had inaugurated the era of the flying clippers. These luxurious planes had seating for 74 (sleeping berths for 36), a separate dining room where passengers were

A postcard showing passengers on a Pan Am flight in 1939.

A Bordo de uno de los Aeropalacios del Sistema PAN AMERICAN AIRWAYS

served full-course meals, dressing rooms, and a lounge. The romantic age of the clippers did not last long. During World War II, the flying boats were all converted into troop and cargo transports. By the end of the war, a new age in aviation, a jet age, was under way.

Tourist Class and the Jet Age

By 1945 Trippe was ready for a new challenge. He realized that further expansion lay not in new routes but in new customers. At that time, world airfares were fixed by a cartel, the International Air Transport Association (IATA). To eliminate competition it feared might weaken the industry, IATA fixed airfares artificially high, and few people could afford to fly.

Trippe introduced a tourist class fare from New York to London, cutting the round-trip fare by more than half, to $275 (about $1,700 in today's dollars). In retaliation, the cartel used its influence to cut Pan Am's routes. Airports were closed to all Pan Am flights with tourist class seats. Trippe found only one route where the cartel could not block him: New York to San Juan, Puerto Rico. Pan Am's one-way fare was $75, and the flights were packed.

By 1952 Trippe's continued attacks on the IATA, coupled with the success of Pan Am, forced the airlines to accept tourist class. The next step for Trippe was to bring tourist class into the jet age. The first commercial jet was the Boeing 707, which first flew in October 1958. The 707 could fly above storms and rough winds, making it capable of flying in most weather conditions. Trippe cut fares, protecting profits by adding more seats.

By the mid-1960s customers were flocking to take advantage of the cheaper fares, and Trippe realized that he needed a larger plane. Trippe turned to Bill Allen, the head of Boeing, saying he wanted a jet two-and-a-half times the size of the 707. According to industry legend, Trippe told Allen, "If you build it, I'll buy it," and Allen responded, "If you buy it, I'll build it." Trippe agreed to buy 25 airplanes, the 747 model, for $450 million.

In 1966 the 747, the plane Trippe helped create, launched the great age of affordable jet

travel, but it also sank Pan Am. Trippe bought too many 747s in the early 1970s. The world oil crisis in the 1970s hit airline travel hard, and his business never recovered. Boeing itself almost went bankrupt from the cost of launching the 747. A decade after Trippe's death in 1981, his airline, already substantially dismembered, finally expired. Trippe had been a continuous innovator, but the sad irony is that he failed to reinvent his company for the leaner, far more competitive age he had done so much to shape.

An employee at John F. Kennedy International Airport in New York takes down the signs after Pan Am's closure in 1991.

Further Reading

Bender, Marylin, and Selig Altschul. *Chosen Instrument: Pan Am, Juan Trippe, the Rise and Fall of an American Entrepreneur.* New York: Simon & Schuster, 1982.

Conrad, Barnaby. *Pan Am: An Aviation Legend.* Emeryville, Calif.: Woodford Press, 1999.

Daley, Robert. *An American Saga: Juan Trippe and His Pan Am Empire.* New York: Random House, 1980.

Fairbairn, Desmond. *Pan Am: Gone but Not Forgotten.* Polo, Ill.: Transportation Trails, 1997.

Gandt, Robert. *Skygods: The Fall of Pan Am.* New York: William Morrow, 1995.

—Lisa Magloff

Trump, Donald

1946–
Real estate mogul

Donald John Trump is one of the richest and most powerful men in the U.S. real estate and casino industries. He is known for his shrewd business sense and his insight into the tastes and preferences of the wealthy.

Trump was born on June 14, 1946, in New York City. He learned early lessons about business from his father, Fred, who had begun his own career by starting a construction business in an attempt to support his family after his father died. As a young man Trump attended a military academy and assisted in the family business. Trump enjoyed the real estate aspects of the business, but he did not like physical labor or other tedious tasks associated with the business as a whole. He eventually studied finance at the University of Pennsylvania's Wharton School of Business. This was a step toward Trump's involvement in real estate on a larger scale; he was determined to make a name for himself in New York's real estate industry.

Nearly broke upon his graduation in 1968, Trump took a job at his father's company, the Trump Organization. Soon after, he moved from his native Queens to a small apartment in Manhattan. To make himself known in the real estate industry, Trump wanted to join an exclusive club where he could meet potential clients. He convinced the manager of the elite Le Club to admit him, and he soon began interacting with fellow members, who included some of New York City's most wealthy residents.

By the 1980s Trump had attained a dominant position in the New York real estate industry, owing in part to his adeptness for securing loans with little collateral. His properties, in addition to several private homes, included Trump Parc, with its 24,000 rental and co-op apartments, and the Plaza Hotel. For a time Trump owned the New Jersey Generals, a United States Football League team. (The team and the league have since gone out of business.) His most famous venture in that decade was the construction of prestigious Trump Tower on Fifth Avenue in Manhattan, completed in 1980. He also built the Trump Shuttle Airline in 1989 and acquired three Atlantic City, New Jersey, casinos (Trump Plaza Hotel and Casino on the Boardwalk, the Trump Marina, and the Taj Mahal) plus a riverboat casino in Indiana.

In all his ventures Trump has seemed to disdain competitive pricing. Even as his competitors lowered prices, Trump raised them. All of his properties, many of them located in prestigious areas of Manhattan, are luxurious. Trump has always believed that the richest people in America, and those who aspire to be like them, do not mind paying extra for opulence and first-class services.

Trump's shrewd deal making could not shield him from financial disaster

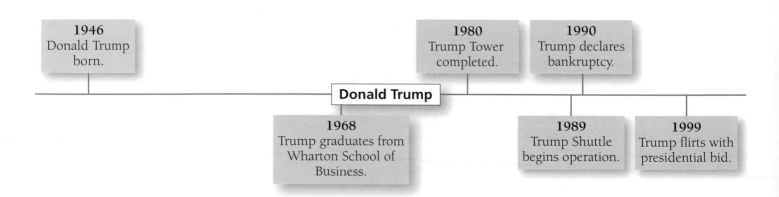

1946
Donald Trump born.

1968
Trump graduates from Wharton School of Business.

Donald Trump

1980
Trump Tower completed.

1989
Trump Shuttle begins operation.

1990
Trump declares bankruptcy.

1999
Trump flirts with presidential bid.

during a recession in 1990, when he was forced into bankruptcy by more than $2 billion in bank loans that he could not repay. Although bondholders and some banks lost millions in their dealings with him, they opted to restructure his debt to avoid additional losses that might result from a court battle. This restructuring of debt saved Trump's empire from total collapse. By 1994 Trump had paid down some of his $900 million personal debt and much of his $3.5 billion business debt. He lost the Trump Shuttle, but he maintained control over his other ventures and has since moved on to new ones. In 1996 he opened a new hotel and office building in New York City. In 2001 he became a codeveloper of the $300 million Ritz-Carlton hotel and residential project in downtown Toronto. The project was his first in Canada.

Trump has also pursued interests outside the real estate industry. He has served as the executive producer of the Miss USA Pageant, which is held in Atlantic City every year, and as the producer of the Miss Universe Pageant. A prominent figure in the U.S. entertainment industry, he has also appeared in a host of television shows and movies.

Despite his earlier statements that he is "too honest" to be a politician, in 1999 Trump announced that he was considering running for president on the Reform Party ticket. Trump's political views have varied: he had previously been a member of the Republican Party and was known for his economic conservatism, but at the same time he had also supported abortion rights, universal health care, a one-time tax of 14.25 percent on the net worth of the superrich (with revenues to be applied to paying down the national debt), and a free trade policy combined with sanctions against countries that refused to open their markets. When Trump turned toward the Reform Party, some observers regarded his move as a serious bid for high office; others took it as an expression of Trump's ego. He soon opted out of the presidential

Donald Trump in New York City in 1999.

campaign, however, and his name never appeared on the ticket. Trump later admitted he might not have made a good politician; he does not like to shake people's hands, he said, since hand-shaking might transmit germs, which is one of his long-time phobias.

Trump's relationships with women have attracted attention in tabloid publications for more than 20 years. His marriage

Donald Trump at the grand opening of his Taj Mahal casino in Atlantic City, New Jersey, in 1990.

to Ivana Trump ended in 1990, after he fathered four children with her. He wed Marla Maples in 1993 and fathered a daughter, Tiffany, before divorcing again in 1999.

Trump is the coauthor of many books, including *Trump: The Art of the Deal* (1988), *Trump: Surviving at the Top* (1990), and *Trump: The Art of the Comeback* (1997). In *The Art of the Comeback,* Trump tells how he was able to rebound from his financial disasters of the early 1990s and subsequently build a net worth of more than $3 billion. He tells readers that going against the tide as he does—for example, by raising prices when his competitors were lowering them—is critical to business success.

Further Reading

Barrett, Wayne, Jonathan Gill, and Timothy L. O'Brien. *Trump: The Deals and the Downfall.* New York: HarperCollins, 1992.

Blair, Gwenda. *The Trumps: Three Generations That Built an Empire.* New York: Simon & Schuster, 2000.

Hurt, Harry. *The Lost Tycoon: The Many Lives of Donald J. Trump.* New York: W. W. Norton, 1993.

Trump, Donald J., with Kate Bohner. *Trump: The Art of the Comeback.* New York: Times Books/Random House, 1997.

Trump, Donald J., with Charles Leerhsen. *Trump: Surviving at the Top.* New York. Random House, 1990.

Trump, Donald J., with Tony Schwartz. *Trump: The Art of the Deal.* Boston, Mass.: G. K. Hall, 1989.

—*Karen Ayres*

Turner, Ted

1938–
Media entrepreneur

See also:
AOL Time Warner; Arts and
Entertainment Industry.

Television pioneer Ted Turner transformed the American television industry during the 1980s when he introduced 24-hour cable news. Turner, known for his philanthropic work, is committed to environmental causes and international programs related to social justice.

Robert Edward Turner III was born in Cincinnati, Ohio, on November 19, 1938. He attended the McCallie School in Chattanooga, Tennessee, where he was a troublemaker, nicknamed "Terrible Ted." He was notorious for practicing taxidermy and growing lawn grass in his room. Turner attended but did not graduate from Brown University, where he was vice president of the debating union.

Turner's professional career began in 1963 when his father, Ed, committed suicide because of problems with the family business, Turner Communications. Young Turner took control of the company, which was centered on billboard advertising. In 1970 he expanded the business into the television industry when he merged with Rice Broadcasting. The deal sealed his control of WTCG, Channel 17, in Atlanta, Georgia.

In 1975 Turner transformed WTCG into cable's first "superstation" to be broadcast by satellite to houses around the country. In 1979 the station was renamed WTBS, and later simply TBS, for Turner Broadcasting System. Featuring plays, movies, and sitcoms, it became the flagship for Turner's entertainment empire. In 1976 Turner bought the Atlanta Braves, a major league baseball team; the following year he purchased the Atlanta Hawks basketball team. The games of both teams were broadcast on TBS.

From the beginning, Turner's controversial and boisterous personality was at the forefront. An avid yachtsman as a young man, he captured the America's Cup in 1977. His bold tactics and confrontational personality earned him the nickname "Captain Outrageous," a label he has retained despite having lost the America's Cup title in 1980.

Building on his success with WTBS, Turner created the Cable News Network (CNN) in 1980. Despite initial skepticism about the market for a 24-hour news network, CNN established itself through its coverage of an assassination attempt on President Ronald Reagan, the 1986 space shuttle disaster, and the Persian Gulf War. In many cases, because of the depth and continuity of its operations, the network was able to obtain news faster than local stations. By 1995 CNN reached 156 million subscribers in 140 countries. The network now offers several channels: CNN Headline News, launched in 1982; CNN International, launched in 1985; CNN Radio; and CNN Airport Network. CNNfn (CNN Financial News) was developed as an economic news channel in 1995. CNN/SI, which merged information from CNN and *Sports Illustrated*, debuted in 1996 as a 24-hour sports news network.

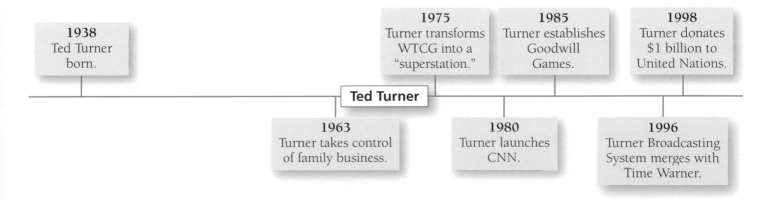

1938
Ted Turner born.

1963
Turner takes control of family business.

1975
Turner transforms WTCG into a "superstation."

Ted Turner

1980
Turner launches CNN.

1985
Turner establishes Goodwill Games.

1996
Turner Broadcasting System merges with Time Warner.

1998
Turner donates $1 billion to United Nations.

Ted Turner in Los Angeles in 1999.

Turner has also experienced some business failures. In 1986 he tried and failed to buy the CBS television network; he purchased Metro-Goldwyn-Mayer, known as MGM/United Artists, instead. He also tried to develop a "Checkout Channel," for people to watch while waiting in line at grocery stores, but the idea was not a success.

In 1985 Turner developed the Goodwill Games, an international competition started as an attempt to involve athletes from the Soviet Union in international competition.

The Soviets had boycotted the Olympic Games, so Turner attempted to create his own substitute version. The first event, held in Moscow in 1986, served as both a publicity stunt for Turner's network and an attempt at fostering international goodwill.

Turner was active in the late 1980s and early 1990s. The cable channel TNT was created in 1988 when Turner's collection of movies and sitcoms increased. Turner unveiled the Cartoon Network in 1992 after he acquired rights to Hanna-Barbera cartoons.

TBS merged with New Line Cinema in 1994 and launched Turner Classic Movies, a 24-hour commercial-free film channel.

Turner made enemies in the film industry when he announced a plan to transform certain black-and-white motion pictures into color copies (a process known as colorizing). Debate surrounding this plan eventually prompted congressional hearings on the ownership and authorship of films. Some film lovers objected to Turner's notion that color would broaden the appeal of the films, arguing that if a film had been made originally in black and white, it should be kept that way out of respect to the filmmakers. Some old films are still colorized, but the practice has largely fallen out of favor.

In possibly the biggest business deal of Turner's career, Turner Broadcasting System merged with Time Warner in 1996, and Turner became the vice chairman of Time Warner. He then served as a vice chairman of newly merged AOL Time Warner, was a member of its board of directors, and owned about 10 percent of the merged company's stock. Nevertheless, industry observers say that Turner lost a considerable amount of power because of the 2000 merger. Turner himself estimates that he has lost between $7 billion and $8 billion as AOL Time Warner stock plummeted following the merger. He announced his retirement in January 2003.

Turner is also president of the Turner Foundation, a charitable organization that has donated money from his immense fortune, which is estimated at several billion dollars, to various causes. For example, in 1994 alone he donated more than $200 million to charity. He generally has targeted his donations to environmental organizations and organizations working for international justice. This was the case in 1998, when he made a $1 billion donation to the United Nations for programs designed to benefit women and children, foster population control, and protect the environment. Altogether, about 450 groups have received funds from the Turner Foundation.

Turner owns about 1.7 million acres of property in the United States. Much of

The CNN newsroom in 2001.

it is ranchland in New Mexico, Montana, Nebraska, Kansas, South Carolina, Florida, and South Dakota. Turner is known for his efforts to preserve the bison that roam on some of these properties.

In 1998 Turner considered running for president, but he abandoned the idea because his then-wife, actress and fitness proponent Jane Fonda, objected. Turner has been married and divorced three times. In 1960 he married Judy Nye, with whom he had one daughter and one son. He married Jane Shirley Smith in 1965 and was divorced from her in 1988 after fathering another daughter and two more sons. He married Fonda in 1991; they divorced in 2001.

Turner holds several honorary degrees. He was named Man of the Year by *Time* magazine in 1991. He remains highly influential in the entertainment world because of his leadership in transforming the television industry and the entertainment business as a whole.

Further Reading

Bibb, Porter. *Ted Turner: It Ain't as Easy as It Looks.* Boulder, Colo.: Johnson Books, 1997.
Schonfeld, Reese. *Me and Ted against the World: The Unauthorized Story of the Founding of CNN.* New York: Cliff Street, 2001.

—*Karen Ayres*

See also:
Fiscal Policy; Inflation; Social Security and Medicare.

Unemployment

Unemployment occurs when a person is not currently working but is able to work and is actively seeking employment. A low level of unemployment is a sign that an economy is strong and healthy, while high levels of unemployment can indicate serious problems in many areas of an economy. For any country as a whole, high levels of unemployment indicate that the productive potential of workers is being lost. For the government, periods of high unemployment result in a loss of tax revenue because workers and families pay fewer taxes when their income is lower.

Unemployment can create a vicious cycle. For unemployed workers and their families, unemployment usually results in a dramatic loss in the wages needed to buy goods and services. Because of this decline in income, unemployed workers are usually forced to cut spending, thus hurting businesses that would have benefited from their patronage. If unemployment becomes widespread, the spending cutbacks can become dramatic, and these businesses may, in turn, be forced to lay off even more workers.

Governments collect data about unemployment in an effort to measure and understand its varied effects. The most important indicator is the unemployment rate. The unemployment rate is the percentage of people in the labor force who are considered unemployed. The labor force is all who are employed or not employed and want to work. People who are not working but also not looking for a job are considered to be out of the labor force. (In some cases, people may be out of work for long periods and give up looking for work; they are called discouraged workers.) The U.S. unemployment rate has varied widely. On a monthly basis, the lowest rate was 2.5 percent in May 1953 and the highest was 10.8 percent in November and December 1982.

Data are also collected on many characteristics of people who are employed and unemployed, including geographic location, industries and occupations, age, sex, and race. Do unemployed people live in a household alone or with children and spouse? Whether unemployment is increasing or decreasing is a key indication of an economy's improvment or decline. All these measures help analysts understand the nature of the unemployment trends in the economy.

Unemployment and the Economy

The unemployment rate is the most widely cited measure of labor market conditions. People often refer to the labor market as tight or loose. A tight labor market has few people who are unemployed; most people who want to find work can do so quickly and employers often have difficulty locating and hiring qualified people. A loose labor market has many people who are unemployed; finding a job can be difficult, and employers can easily fill open positions. Historically an unemployment rate of 5 percent was considered tight and a rate of about 7 percent was considered loose.

One of the most important ways that unemployment affects the economy as a whole is by increasing or decreasing inflationary pressures—the prices of goods and

Unemployment Rates by Industry 1980 to 2000
(in percent)

	1980	1985	1990[1]	1995[1]	2000[1]
All unemployed [2]	7.1	7.2	5.6	5.6	4.0
Industry: [3]					
Agriculture	11.0	13.2	9.8	11.1	7.5
Mining	6.4	9.5	4.8	5.2	3.9
Construction	14.1	13.1	11.1	11.5	6.4
Manufacturing	8.5	7.7	5.8	4.9	3.6
Transportation and public utilities	4.9	5.1	3.9	4.5	3.1
Wholesale and retail trade	7.4	7.6	6.4	6.5	5.0
Finance, insurance, and real estate	3.4	3.5	3.0	3.3	2.3
Services	5.9	6.2	5.0	5.4	3.8
Government	4.1	3.9	2.7	2.9	2.0

Note: Rate represents unemployment as a percent of labor force in each specified group.
[1] Data not strictly comparable with data for earlier years. [2] Includes the self-employed, unpaid family workers, and persons with no previous work experience, not shown separately. [3] Covers unemployed wage and salary workers.
Source: U.S. Bureau of Labor Statistics, *Employment and Earnings*, January issues, 1980 to 2000.

services. When unemployment is low and the market is considered tight, workers are not only more likely to have a job but also more able to demand pay increases in the jobs that they have, and employers are less able to resist. In response, businesses often raise the prices of their goods or services to be able to pay the higher salaries. Similarly, as more workers are employed and those who have jobs are more able to demand wage increases, they are better able to pay increasing prices.

By contrast, when unemployment is high, workers are less able to demand higher wages because they are glad to have any job. Similarly, as more people are unemployed, they are less able to spend on consumer goods. Businesses are forced to keep prices steady.

Generally this market dynamic for unemployment seems to hold true. However, some periods seem to be notable exceptions. For example, during the 1970s, both inflation and unemployment rates were high. During the 1990s, unemployment was quite low, but upward pressure on prices was absent.

Types of Unemployment

Economists have identified four types of unemployment: frictional unemployment, cyclical unemployment, structural unemployment, and seasonal unemployment. These each have different qualities and different causes.

Frictional unemployment (because transitions between jobs are rarely smooth) is thought to be relatively short-term unemployment when workers find themselves between jobs. Individuals can lose a job by being fired, being laid off, quitting, or for other reasons. When any of these happens,

A protest against unemployment in New York City in 1909.

some time may be needed to find a new job. Short delays are considered friction in the labor market. Some amount of frictional unemployment is always present as some people always experience short delays between jobs.

Cyclical unemployment is caused by a deeper downturn in the economy as a whole. It affects a large number of people who may face a longer period of unemployment. When the business cycle turns downward, demand for goods and services drops as a result, and workers are laid off. Because the entire economy is suffering, workers often have difficulty finding new jobs.

Structural unemployment results from a mismatch between the skills of workers and the skills needed by employers. This can occur in a particular geographic area or during a specific time. Technological advances, for example, often cause businesses to need workers with new skills to take advantage of the technology. People without those skills can find themselves unemployed. Structural unemployment can also affect a geographic area where a plant or business closes down or moves and lays off its workers.

Seasonal unemployment primarily affects workers in the agricultural and construction industries. In the winter months, for example, jobs associated with fruit harvesting and new home construction disappear in some regions until the weather improves. Students often look for work during their summer vacations. If they do not find jobs, they are also usually considered seasonally unemployed.

Employment and Government Policy
Workers who lose their jobs through no fault of their own can receive unemployment

Unemployment by Occupation 1990 to 2000

	Number (in thousands)			Unemployment rate		
	1990	1995	2000	1990	1995	2000
Executive, administrative, and managerial	350	420	356	2.3	2.4	1.8
Professional specialty	316	460	369	2.0	2.5	1.7
Total, executive, managerial, and professional	666	880	725	2.1	2.4	1.7
Technicians and related support	116	113	97	2.9	2.8	2.2
Sales occupations	720	795	684	4.8	5.0	4.0
Administrative support, including clerical	804	836	684	4.1	4.3	3.5
Total, technical, sales, and administrative support	1,641	1,744	1,464	4.3	4.5	3.6
Private household	47	99	58	5.6	10.7	6.9
Protective service	74	86	65	3.6	3.7	2.6
Service except private household and protective	1,018	1,193	900	7.1	7.9	5.6
Total, service occupations	1,139	1,378	1,023	6.6	7.5	5.3
Mechanics and repairers	175	182	129	3.8	4.0	2.6
Construction trades	483	501	312	8.5	9.0	4.9
Other precision production, craft, and repair	202	177	113	4.7	4.2	2.8
Total, precision production, craft, and repair	861	860	554	5.9	6.0	3.6
Machine operators, assemblers, inspectors	727	629	455	8.1	7.4	5.9
Transportation and moving occupations	329	329	253	6.3	6.0	4.4
Handlers, equipment cleaners, helpers, laborers	657	660	520	11.6	11.7	8.7
Total, operators, fabricators, and laborers	1,714	1,618	1,228	8.7	8.2	6.3
Farming, forestry, and fishing	237	311	215	6.4	7.9	6.0
Total unemployed[1]	7,047	7,404	5,655	5.6	5.6	4.0

[1] Includes persons with no previous work experience and those whose last job was in the armed forces.
Source: U.S. Bureau of Labor Statistics, *Employment and Earnings,* January issues, 1990 to 2000.

benefits from their state. These payments cover a percentage of the worker's previous salary. However, a particular worker is not necessarily eligible to collect unemployment. Eligibility is keyed to an employee having worked a minimum number of weeks, which varies widely by state. The amount of the benefit, which is subject to a cap, is based on a percentage of the employee's salary earned over a specified period. The employer supports the insurance program through premiums based on its payroll. Workers can typically receive unemployment checks for up to 26 weeks, except in times of recession when the federal government may allow states to provide extended benefits. To continue to receive benefits, unemployed workers must demonstrate that they are actively seeking work but have not been able to find a job.

Unemployment insurance (UI) principally provides some financial cushion to people who lose their jobs. Without unemployment insurance, workers who face even short periods of unemployment may become impoverished. UI also helps the economy as a whole by enabling people to continue to spend money and fuel business activity.

When looking at government policies on unemployment and employment, economists are often interested in evaluating their effect on labor market flexibility. A flexible labor market is one in which people move easily in and out of jobs. For UI, economists seek a balance between providing a financial cushion for unemployed workers and providing so much money that workers will have little incentive to find a new job. If unemployed workers are provided substantial UI checks over a long period, the fear is that they will simply live off their unemployment checks and not try hard to find new employment. Thus UI is sometimes considered to be a barrier to a flexible labor market. Policy makers can have very different opinions about how to strike a balance between supporting workers' income and creating incentives for them to find new work.

Measuring Unemployment

In the United States, unemployment-related data are primarily collected by the Bureau of Labor Statistics (BLS), a division of the U.S. Department of Labor. On the first Friday of every month, BLS releases the results of its survey. These data include the total number of employed and unemployed persons for the previous month.

The data are gathered from a monthly survey, *Current Population Survey* (CPS), which has been conducted every month since 1940. The survey consists of responses from 60,000 households in the United States. The sample is selected to be representative of the entire population of the United States.

The survey asks about the employment status of each person in the household over the age of 15. People are considered employed if they did any work during that week for pay or profit, worked 15 hours or more as an unpaid worker in a family business, or were temporarily absent from a job. People are considered unemployed if they do not have a job, have actively looked for work in the prior four weeks, and are currently available for work. Actively looking for work is defined as any of the following:
- contacting an employer
- having a job interview
- meeting with a public, private, school, or university employment counselor
- talking with friends or relatives about job possibilities
- sending out resumes or filling out applications
- placing or answering advertisements
- checking union or professional registers
- some other means of active job search

For workers who have jobs, a balance must be struck between protecting them from sudden changes in the economy or unfair treatment from employers, while providing employers the flexibility to have the best workers when they are needed. In some countries, employers face barriers to firing employees whose performance is substandard or employees whose skills are no longer required. These are sometimes considered signs of an inflexible labor market. Here, too, policy makers differ widely on where to strike the right balance.

Further Reading

Bix, Amy Sue. *Inventing Ourselves Out of Jobs?: America's Debate over Technological Unemployment.* Baltimore, Md.: Johns Hopkins University Press, 2000.

Eatwell, John, ed. *Global Unemployment: Loss of Jobs in the '90s.* Armonk, N.Y.: M. E. Sharpe, 1996.

Standing, Guy. *Beyond the New Paternalism: Basic Security as Equality.* London and New York: Verso, 2002.

—*Carl Haacke*

Union Bank of Switzerland

Although a product of 125 years of Swiss banking history, the Union Bank of Switzerland (UBS AG) was formed only in 1997, when Swiss Banking Corporation (SBC) acquired its larger rival, Union Bank of Switzerland (UBS). The new company, UBS AG, is one of the 10 largest banks in the world and the largest bank in Europe.

The Union Bank of Switzerland provides financial services through four divisions. Its UBS AG Switzerland unit includes its consumer and corporate banking in Switzerland as well as its private banking services. UBS Asset Management offers individual and institutional asset management, mutual funds, and other services. The company's UBS Warburg (formerly Warburg Dillon Read) provides corporate finance, investment banking, and other investment services. In 2000 UBS bought American investment broker Paine Webber.

The Union Bank of Switzerland and SBC were originally founded more than 100 years ago as joint-stock banks. A joint-stock bank is a group of people who pool their money (share capital) to invest. The company issues shares and acts as a single entity for the purposes of investment.

Joint-stock banks were used to help fund the construction of railway lines and the industrialization of Switzerland. The origin of SBC dates to 1854, when a consortium of six private banking houses, called Bankverein, was founded to act as an underwriting syndicate. The following year, the Bank in Winterthur, the predecessor of UBS, was formed. Bankverein was later re-formed as a joint-stock company under the name Basler Bankverein (1871). Both banks became heavily involved with financing the building of Swiss railways.

In the late nineteenth and early twentieth centuries, both the Basler Bankverein and the Bank in Winterthur underwent a series of mergers and consolidations. Basler

Union Bank of Switzerland

1854
Consortium of six private banking houses (or Bankverein) established to form an underwriting syndicate, the origin of Swiss Banking Corporation (SBC).

1855
Bank in Winterthur, predecessor of Union Bank of Switzerland (UBS), established.

1871
Bankverein re-formed as a joint-stock company, renamed Basler Bankverein.

1896
Basler Bankverein formed into Schweizerischer Bankverein (Swiss Bank Company).

1921
The English name Union Bank of Switzerland (UBS) adopted.

1930s
Both Nazis and Jews make use of Swiss banks.

1997
Security guard Christoph Meili discovers World War II–era UBS documents.

1997
SBC and UBS merge to form Union Bank of Switzerland (UBS AG).

1999
Volcker Committee issues report clearing Swiss banks of intentionally embezzling assets of Holocaust victims.

2000
Global shares of UBS AG begin trading on the New York Stock Exchange.

The headquarters of UBS in Zurich in 1998.

Bankverein emerged in 1896 as the Schweizerischer Bankverein (Swiss Bank Company). The Bank of Winterthur eventually formed the Schweizerische Bankgesellschaft (Union of Swiss Banks). Its English name was changed to Union Bank of Switzerland in 1921.

Over the following decades, the two banks continued to grow, becoming two of the largest banks in Switzerland. However, UBS suffered severe losses in the 1990s, following a series of loan defaults by banks and governments in Southeast Asia, Russia, and Latin America. UBS was also one of the principal investors in the Greenwich, Connecticut–based fund, Long-Term Capital Management. The fund's poor management and near collapse cost UBS $780 million, and left it open for takeover.

The End of Secrecy?

Swiss banks have always brought with them a certain mystique because of Switzerland's banking laws, which allow for great secrecy. Under Swiss law, tax evasion is not a crime, and as Switzerland is not a member of the European Union, it does not have to follow European banking rules, which make assisting tax evasion a crime. Swiss banks also adhere to extensive secrecy laws, which prevent them from disclosing financial information of account holders to Swiss or foreign governments. In the past, money lodged with Swiss banks could not be frozen or confiscated by foreign governments. Foreign governments had a very difficult time investigating money that was passed through Swiss banks for the purpose of "laundering."

Since their establishment, Swiss banks have been used to avoid taxes and investigations on both legally and illegally acquired money. This constant inflow of money has kept Swiss interest rates among the lowest in the world and helped boost the Swiss standard of living.

Swiss banks have come under increasing scrutiny as governments seek to trace the movement of money used to fund criminal enterprises and terrorism. As international pressure mounts, the banks are being forced to cooperate with foreign governments. One of the turning points in opening up Swiss banking involved USB. During World War II, Nazi leaders used Swiss banks to stash money earned from forced sales of Jewish property and earned by businesses using slave labor. In addition, in the late 1930s many Jewish families had deposited money in Swiss accounts, hoping to keep it safe from the Nazis. At the end of the war, Swiss banks refused to help find stolen money hidden in their banks. More important, they also refused to release the money held in dormant Jewish accounts, often claiming the money was not traceable or could not be released without proper documentation.

In 1997 UBS security guard Christoph Meili discovered a pile of prewar banking documents in the UBS archives division, about to go into a shredder. The documents indicated that the bank knew exactly where to find the money of Jewish account holders it had claimed did not exist. After Meili alerted investigators, he was arrested by Swiss authorities for violating Swiss banking secrecy laws, but the ensuing legal battles eventually led to an agreement between Swiss banks and Jewish groups for $1.2 billion in restitution. (Meili subsequently moved to the United States.) In addition, UBS was forced to release information about more than 2,000 dormant accounts.

The Volcker Committee (an independent investigative committee) issued a final report in 1999 clearing Swiss banks of intentionally embezzling the assets of Holocaust victims. The UBS case and the subsequent agreement have helped pave the way for more cooperation between foreign governments and Swiss banking authorities.

These developments have hurt Switzerland's reputation as a place to stash ill-gotten gains, but they have not hurt the earnings of UBS AG. Following initial losses directly after the merger, the new company quickly regained its standing as Europe's top bank. The bank handles assets for more than four million private and corporate clients and has credit ratings among the highest of any bank. Global shares in UBS AG began trading on the New York Stock Exchange (NYSE) in 2000. UBS AG is the first non–U.S. financial services group to list its Global Registered Shares directly on the NYSE, thus positioning itself to play an even larger role in world finance in the future.

In 1997 Holocaust survivor Alice Fischer looks through papers that she believes connect her to money held in Swiss bank accounts since World War II.

Further Reading

Bauer, Hans, and Warren J. Blackman. *Swiss Banking: An Analytical History*. New York: St. Martin's Press, 1998.

Faith, Nicholas. *Safety in Numbers: The Mysterious World of Swiss Banking*. London: Hamish Hamilton, 1982.

Ziegler, Jean. *How Swiss Bankers Helped Finance the Nazi War Machine*. San Diego, Calif.: Harcourt Brace, 1998.

—*Lisa Magloff*

United Automobile Workers of America

Formally named the International Union, United Automobile, Aerospace, and Agricultural Implement Workers of America (UAW), the UAW represents automotive and other vehicular workers. It also represents a wide variety of other workers in manufacturing, technical fields, and the professions.

The UAW was born out of the conflict between craft unions and industrial unions. Although union organizing had gained momentum in the United States during the 1920s and early 1930s, most of the unions, including the nation's largest union, the American Federation of Labor (AFL), still represented primarily skilled workers. At the 1935 AFL convention, leaders of the industrial unions established the Committee of Industrial Organizations (CIO) within the AFL. Several small industrial unions then merged to establish the UAW as an affiliate of the CIO.

At the 1936 AFL convention, arguments broke out as the "old guard" craft faction tried to reduce the previous year's commitment to organize mass-production industries. The old guard won and the AFL suspended the unskilled labor unions affiliated with the CIO. The suspended unions formed the Congress of Industrial Organizations, the new CIO. The UAW, always uncomfortable with the AFL's insistence on selecting the UAW's leadership and dictating its organizing strategy, quickly joined the new CIO.

Organizing Auto Workers

The UAW was eager to begin organizing the automobile plants, the largest pool of unskilled laborers in the nation. It decided to start with General Motors (GM), the nation's largest industrial employer. In the fall of 1936 autoworkers began staging sit-down strikes at various GM plants. Their demands included a 30-hour week; a six-hour day; overtime pay; a minimum wage; promotion based on length of employment; and recognition of the UAW as the sole bargaining agency for GM employees.

The strikes soon spread and GM's Fisher Body plants in Flint, Michigan, became the main battleground. Located 60 miles northwest of Detroit, Flint was a virtual company town. The mayor, police chief, and three city commissioners—as well as Flint's newspaper, radio station, and school officials—were all on the GM payroll. Four of every five workers in the city were employed at GM's Chevrolet, Buick, Fisher Body, and AC Spark Plug plants.

GM tried repeatedly to break the strike. On January 11, 1937, sheriff's deputies and police stormed Flint's Chevrolet Plant 2.

See also:
AFL-CIO; Collective Bargaining; Labor Union; National Labor Relations Act; Strikes.

United Automobile Workers of America

1935
United Automobile Workers (UAW) established.

1937
GM, the country's largest manufacturer, agrees to allow union organizing.

1939
UAW joins new Congress of Industrial Organizations and begins staging strikes at various General Motors (GM) factories.

1941
UAW and Ford sign first collective bargaining agreement.

1973
OPEC oil embargo causes decline in American automobile industry.

2002
UAW has 700,000 active members in the United States, Canada, and Puerto Rico.

Strikers repelled the assault by using the plant's fire hoses and raining two-pound car hinges down on the police. Later that night the police returned and were driven back a second time. Humiliated and angry, police opened fire, wounding several strikers. After the failure of a third charge, at midnight, the police gave up and left. The next morning, Flint workers lined up two abreast at UAW headquarters to sign membership cards and pay dues.

By early February the situation at Flint had reached a stalemate and union leaders decided to try a ruse. The UAW announced plans to take over GM's Chevrolet Plant 9. When GM moved all its guards to Plant 9, the union took over nearby Chevrolet Plant 4, the sole source of engines for Chevrolet's entire car line.

UAW-CIO Puts Wheels on the USA

I was standing down on Gratiot Street one
  day,
When I thought I overheard a soldier say,
"Every tank and plane in camp
Carries the UAW stamp
And I am UAW too. I'm proud to say."
It's that UAW-CIO
Makes that army roll and go,
Turnin' out jeeps and tanks and airplanes
  every day.
It's that UAW-CIO
Makes that army roll and go—
Puts wheels on the U.S.A.
I was there on that cold December day
When we heard about Pearl Harbor far
  away;
I was down at Cadillac Square
When the union rallied there
To put them plans for pleasure cars away.
It's that UAW-CIO
Makes that army roll and go,
Turnin' out jeeps and tanks and airplanes
  every day.
It's that UAW-CIO
Makes that army roll and go—
Puts wheels on the U.S.A.
There'll be a union label in Berlin
When the union boys in uniform march in;
And rolling in the ranks
There'll be UAW tanks
—Roll Hitler out and roll the union in!

Source: Anti-Fascist Songs of the Almanac Singers, 1942

On February 13, 1937, with car production at a near-standstill and its share of the automobile market plummeting, GM agreed to negotiate. The company acknowledged the UAW as bargaining agent for its members, agreed to drop all related lawsuits, and to refrain from disciplining the strikers. All other UAW demands would be discussed in a national labor–management conference. Although most of the strike demands had yet to be won, the victory was enormous. The country's largest manufacturer had agreed to allow union organizing. Other industries soon followed.

In March, Chrysler workers won union recognition. Later in the year, workers at North American Aviation (now Rockwell International) and J. I. Case won the right to be represented by the UAW, becoming the first collective bargaining agreements in the aircraft and agricultural implement industries.

The last of the "Big Three" automakers to be organized was the Ford Motor Company. Henry Ford had formed the Ford Service Department to intimidate, spy, and use force to prevent unionizing. On March 27, 1937, members of the Ford Service Department attacked and beat UAW organizers who were handing out union handbills on an overpass leading to a Ford plant. When photos of the "Battle of the Overpass" were printed in the newspapers, sympathy for Ford evaporated. Witnesses testified before the National Labor Relations Board, which ordered Ford to stop interfering with union organization. In June 1941, following a successful strike, the UAW and Ford signed the first collective bargaining agreement at the company.

The UAW during and after World War II

When the United States entered World War II, the UAW adopted a "no strike" pledge for the duration of the war to ensure that the war effort was not hindered by work stoppages. The ability of America's industry to pump out planes and tanks was an important factor in the winning of the war. By the end of the war, industrial unions had become symbols of American strength.

Robert Johnson, right, of Chicago, director of Region Four, with UAW president Walter Reuther after the latter was elected unanimously to his seventh term in 1957.

An early member of the UAW, Walter Reuther became its president in 1946, a job he would hold until his death in 1970. Reuther's philosophy, sometimes called "business unionism" or simply "Reutherism," was that unions should take a militant stance if necessary, but only on so-called pocketbook issues like wages, job security, and benefits. Reuther eschewed any challenge to management's control of the means of production; in this sense, the politics of the UAW were American liberal-democratic, not European socialist, and certainly not communist. This approach, and management's willingness to share profits at a time of unprecedented prosperity, was the cornerstone of the postwar accord between business and labor. This new spirit of cooperation led to more union victories, even as politicians chipped away at union power with legislation like the Taft–Hartley Act of 1947.

Membership in the UAW continued to grow alongside America's automobile industry. In the 1960s and 1970s, UAW members won fully paid hospitalization and sick leave benefits, profit sharing at American Motors, early retirement at Harvester, and shorter hours at Caterpillar. The UAW also bargained for and won long-term contracts, providing a previously unknown level of job security. These gains established a pattern that the union was able to extend to the rest of the auto industry, and eventually to agricultural implement, aerospace, and many independent manufacturers of parts.

Problems for the UAW

During the late 1970s and early 1980s, the American automobile industry fell on tough

UAW members effectively shut down the General Motors fabricating plant in Flint, Michigan, during a 1998 strike.

flexibility and "leanness" with minimal argument over the means of achieving it. Critics dubbed this philosophy, in this and other industries, "concession bargaining." The UAW's cooperation with the auto industry led to a 1985 exodus of the Canadian branch of UAW in protest of the moderation of the national leadership.

The UAW, like other unions, has always been involved in national politics. Union leadership has consistently endorsed Democratic Party candidates and campaigned vigorously against both Ronald Reagan and George Bush. However, the UAW's power to guarantee Democrats the votes of its huge membership has waned. Many UAW members now vote Republican. With union membership down, the UAW has also lost a lot of its clout in Congress. Although the UAW campaigned heavily against the North American Free Trade Agreement, it gained few concessions. Many companies still argue that union demands leave U.S. companies unable to compete.

Nevertheless, the UAW remains a powerful force in the manufacturing industries. Although the UAW is most famous for its association with the auto industry, in fact the union represents a wide variety of workers, including casino employees, food-processing workers, and makers of musical instruments. The Technical, Office, and Professional branch of the UAW represents writers, industrial designers, librarians, and teaching assistants, among others. In 2002 the UAW had more than 950 local unions representing 700,000 active members.

times. The OPEC oil embargo led to fuel shortages and skyrocketing prices. Many consumers started buying more fuel-efficient imported cars. By 1979 employers were demanding concessions from the UAW at the bargaining table. Companies complained that union demands were responsible for high costs that left them unable to compete with cheaper imports. The union resisted concessions at General Motors, Ford, and Harvester, but the workers at Chrysler agreed to concessions that led to federally guaranteed loans, which saved Chrysler from bankruptcy. The UAW also cooperated with restructuring programs set in motion to try to make the industry more competitive.

For better or for worse, the UAW took a fairly conservative, defensive position toward the industrial restructuring of the 1980s and early 1990s. Union leadership sought primarily to limit the massive hemorrhage of jobs; this led to the UAW becoming, in a sense, a subordinate "junior partner" with management, embracing management's project of

Further Reading

Boyle, Kevin. *The UAW and the Heyday of American Liberalism, 1945–1968.* Ithaca, N.Y.: Cornell University Press, 1998.

Buffa, Dudley. *Union Power and American Democracy: The UAW and the Democratic Party, 1935–72.* Ann Arbor: University of Michigan Press, 1984.

Kraus, Henry, and Nelson Lichtenstein. *Heroes of Unwritten Story: The UAW, 1934–39.* Urbana: University of Illinois Press, 1994.

Reuther, Victor. *The Brothers Reuther and the Story of the UAW.* Boston: Houghton Mifflin, 1976.

—Lisa Magloff

United States Steel Corporation

At the time of its formation in 1901, United States Steel Corporation was of such preeminence in American industry that it was known simply as "the Corporation." Men of means and vision anticipated the potential of steel production and dared to imagine a huge conglomerate of industrial manufacturers assembled into one organization. Together, they assembled U.S. Steel and, in so doing, launched the largest company in the world.

The Founding of U.S. Steel

In the last half of the nineteenth century, iron's dominance of the metal industry was giving way to steel production. This new and upcoming manufacturing process was open to expansion and innovation. The introduction of steamships and the expansion of railroads allowed for ore and steel products to flow efficiently over hundreds of miles from mines to manufacturer to consumer. The latest inventions and scientific discoveries were used in steel produc tion and its applications; the result was numerous ancillary industries whose existence depended on attaining and holding a piece of the steel production market.

Work in the steel industry was grueling. Miners and factory workers toiled to exhaustion and often collapsed at a young age from the effects of coal dust, blast furnace heat, and backbreaking labor. At the same time, managers and executives fought ruthlessly for the largest profits. With stakes so high, competition was bitter and pricing unscrupulous. Those entrepreneurs who succeeded amassed great fortunes; others sacrificed everything only to end in financial ruin.

In the late 1800s the Carnegie Steel Company was foremost in the industry. When Andrew Carnegie decided to retire in 1900, he persuaded financier J. P. Morgan to purchase his company. Carnegie suggested that to maintain control of the industry, Morgan should assemble a steel conglomerate of contributing industries. Morgan complied, forming U.S. Steel, a giant holding company and the world's first billion-dollar corporation.

The financial world gasped at the size of Morgan's venture, capitalized with more than $1 billion in stock and $304 million in bonds. People had difficulty conceiving of a billion (one thousand million). One report told readers to imagine $1 bills connected end to end circling the Earth six times and leaving two 8,000-mile streamers floating behind—quite a concept considering that one dollar would buy four steak dinners. Critics questioned the wisdom of financing an endeavor at a cost exceeding its assets. Some predicted the stock was doomed to fail, while others argued that the value of the corporation was in its earning potential, an

See also:
Carnegie, Andrew;
Manufacturing Industry;
Monopoly; Morgan, J. P.

United States Steel Corporation

1901
J. P. Morgan buys Carnegie Steel Co. and creates United States Steel Corporation.

1920
U.S. Steel cleared of monopoly charges by U.S. Supreme Court.

1982
U.S. Steel diversifies and restructures, acquiring Marathon Oil Company.

1986
U.S. Steel changes its name to USX.

2001
Steel-related portion of USX is broken off from parent company, renamed U.S. Steel.

In 1948 the first steel beams for the United Nations Secretariat Building are loaded at the Homestead Works of U.S. Steel's Carnegie–Illinois Steel Corporation, where they were rolled. They will be shipped to a fabrication plant where they will be made into sections; the beams will then be sent to New York.

amount they believed would eventually exceed its assets. After all, they said, the value of the island of Manhattan, purchased for just $24, had been in its potential for future earnings.

Morgan and Carnegie are said to have discussed that matter of money some time later aboard a cruise ship crossing the Atlantic. According to legend, Carnegie boasted of his shrewdness in making the deal for such a large sum, to which Morgan replied that he would have paid a hundred million more.

Running U.S. Steel

Elbert H. Gary subsequently took over leadership of the steel industry. A lawyer who earlier had been asked to leave his practice to head Federal Steel Company in Chicago, Gary felt that Federal's plant was neither sufficiently large nor appropriately located for his purposes. He had petitioned Morgan for expansion and relocation money about the same time Carnegie was pursuing Morgan as an investor. When Morgan incorporated U.S. Steel, Gary's plant was included in the deal.

Carnegie and Gary were both men of great ambition, but their backgrounds and leadership styles differed. Carnegie, a smart and talented Scots immigrant ironworker, worked up through the ranks to build an industrial empire over which he reigned supreme. His interests were national, and, except for wartime efforts, he had avoided overseas markets. Gary had been handed his leadership role and looked beyond his own power, envisioning a highly principled company with worker ownership and worldwide operations.

Once part of the U.S. Steel board of directors, Gary pressed his philosophy. "The Corporation," he argued, invited disapproval and legal attack because its size was threatening and intimidating. Only through an open policy of goodwill, he maintained, would the nation be convinced that this powerful behemoth could be beneficial. Eventually he won over the staunch opposition of the Morgan camp. In time, cutthroat competitive practices were discontinued, the company offered stock to employees, and markets were opened to the rest of the world. Gary's approach helped U.S. Steel defend itself from charges of antitrust activity and convinced the U.S. Supreme Court in 1920 that the holding company had not behaved like a monopoly.

In its first year U.S. Steel produced two-thirds of the nation's steel and 30 percent of steel made worldwide, but that supremacy declined throughout the century. The corporation's size grew to be problematic—hierarchical, top-down management that worked

well in the beginning was clumsy and inefficient in the faster-paced economy that evolved in the twentieth century. Foreign and domestic competition began to infringe on its markets. U.S. Steel adjusted and adapted in relatively minor ways until 1982, when the company restructured its finances and diversified its markets significantly. Acquiring Marathon Oil Company, one of the nation's largest oil companies, U.S. Steel added financial resources and expanded into the energy industry.

The merged companies signified their unity in 1986 when they changed their name to USX, but the association did not last. In October 2001 the portion of the company concentrating on steel and steel-related businesses broke off from USX, resuming the name of U.S. Steel. Operating out of headquarters in Pittsburgh, Pennsylvania, U.S. Steel manufactures a wide variety of steel and tin products plus coke and taconite pellets. In 2002, more than 100 years after its formation, U.S. Steel produced less than 10 percent of the nation's steel and less than 2 percent of global steel output.

Further Reading

Cotter, Arundel. *United States Steel: A Corporation with a Soul.* Garden City, N.Y.: Doubleday, Page, 1921.

Warren, Kenneth. *Big Steel: The First Century of the United States Steel Corporation, 1901–2001.* Pittsburgh, Pa.: University of Pittsburgh Press, 2001.

—*Karen Ehrle*

An employee of the USX Edgar Thomson Works in Braddock, Pennsylvania, fills ingot molds with new molten steel in 1990.

See also:
AT&T; Energy Industry;
Enron; Standard Oil;
Telecommunications
Industry.

Utilities Industry

The utilities industry is a broadly defined group of businesses that can be roughly divided into three sectors: electric and natural gas, telephone and cable television, and water. Although the companies that operate in these businesses vary widely in size and ownership, all provide essential services to residential and commercial users. Public utilities often operate as a monopoly, serving an exclusive territory or customer base. Accordingly, public utilities are closely regulated by federal, state, or local governments, which try to ensure that these companies serve the public interest and avoid charging exorbitant prices for their services. Since the 1980s a trend toward easing government monitoring has grown, posing both opportunities and problems for the utilities industry.

Electric and Natural Gas

Although electricity has been the subject of scientific study for centuries, using electricity for residential and commercial purposes became popular only following the perfection of the electric motor and light bulb in the late nineteenth century. Likewise, natural gas has been an important energy source in the United States only since the discovery of oil in Pennsylvania in 1859. Because electricity and gas are integral to the lives of all Americans and the national economy, the companies that provide these resources are among the largest in the country and control billions of dollars in assets. Electric and gas utilities serve territories ranging in size from a city or county to most of an entire state. Although the majority of these businesses are privately owned corporations, several large utilities (Los Angeles Department of Water & Power, for example) are operated by the municipalities they serve.

The majority of electric companies generate their own electricity that is sold to customers over lines they control. The power is generated using a variety of fuels, including coal, natural gas, nuclear, water, and renewable sources like solar and wind. A growing number of utilities do not generate the majority of their power internally, but rather buy power from other companies. Natural gas companies generally operate in a slightly different manner. One segment of this industry focuses on extracting natural gas and transporting it through pipelines for resale to local natural gas utilities. These local companies then distribute the gas to the end users. Some companies, for example, Pacific Gas and Electric, distribute both electricity and natural gas.

Telephone and Cable Television

Because the telephone is an essential element of personal communications, telephone

Residential Electricity and Natural Gas: Consumption, Expenditures, and Average Price 1980 to 1997

	Units	1980	1983	1985	1987	1990	1997
Consumption							
Natural Gas	Quad. Btu.[1]	5.31	4.77	4.98	4.83	4.86	5.28
Electricity	Quad. Btu.[1]	2.42	2.42	2.48	2.76	3.03	3.54
Expenditure							
Natural Gas	$ bil.	17.8	27.1	29.8	26.1	27.3	35.8
Electricity	$ bil.	32.6	48.4	54.5	61.6	71.5	88.3
Average Price							
Natural Gas	$/mil. btu	3.36	5.67	5.97	5.41	5.60	6.78
Electricity	$/mil. btu	13.46	19.98	21.94	22.34	23.60	24.97

[1]One quadrillion British thermal units.
Source: U.S. Bureau of the Census, *Statistical Abstracts of the United States,* 2001,
http://www.census.gov/prod/2002pubs/01statab/inforcomm.pdf (April 29, 2003).

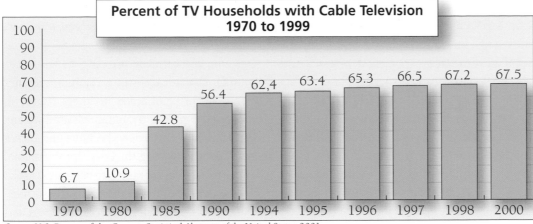

Percent of TV Households with Cable Television 1970 to 1999

Year	Percent
1970	6.7
1980	10.9
1985	42.8
1990	56.4
1994	62.4
1995	63.4
1996	65.3
1997	66.5
1998	67.2
2000	67.5

Source: U.S. Bureau of the Census, *Statistical Abstracts of the United States,* 2001.
http://www.census.gov/prod/2002pubs/01statab/inforcomm.pdf (April 9, 2003).

companies are often considered to be public utilities. Unlike other sectors of the utilities industry, however, the telephone industry has historically been dominated by one company—Bell Telephone and its parent, AT&T. Founded by Alexander Graham Bell one year after he invented the telephone in 1876, Bell Telephone led the development of local and long-distance telephone service in the United States, and by 1915 it had established the first transcontinental telephone lines. Bell Telephone, however, was not the sole provider of telephone service; during the early 1900s a number of smaller companies formed to provide local telephone service. Because the different telephone companies had established no interconnection between their systems, subscribers of one company could not call customers of another company. In 1913 the federal government entered into an agreement with AT&T in which AT&T agreed to connect noncompeting independent telephone companies to its network; in exchange the company was allowed to operate as a legally sanctioned monopoly regulated by the government.

Traditionally, phone companies were responsible for building and maintaining the lines and switching equipment necessary to transmit calls. They also provided customer services like operators and telephone books. The growth of new technologies since the 1960s, however, has radically altered the nature of the telephone industry. Computer automation has greatly improved the quality and reliability of telephone service; satellites and cell phones have made communication possible from virtually anywhere. One result is that the dominance of AT&T has effectively ended as new companies have entered the telephone business to provide these new services.

Cable television involves the transmission of television signals over coaxial cables to individual subscribers. First appearing in the late 1940s, cable systems expanded rapidly in the 1970s not only because cable offered better reception than traditional antennas, but also because cable networks like Home Box Office began providing programming

Careers in the Utilities Industry

As utilities provide a vital public service, careers in the utility industry have the advantage of relative stability. Once the necessary skills have been mastered, an individual has some assurance that he or she can always obtain a job.

A college degree is not a requirement for entry-level utilities jobs; however, employers generally seek applicants with an aptitude for science, mathematics, or mechanics. Most utility employers have come to rely on computers to help perform their services, particularly within the telecommunications industry, and certain jobs in the utilities sector may require a high degree of technical knowledge and skill. Most utilities employers provide on-the-job training; certain jobs may require a period of apprenticeship.

Although many jobs within the utilities industry are not physically strenuous, certain occupations within the industry can be quite hazardous, particularly those involved in the repair and maintenance of utilities structures, including gas lines and electric power cables. As utilities are a 24-hour service, utilities workers usually work either one of three 8-hour or one of two 12-hour shifts on a rotating basis. Such rotating shifts can cause disruptions in sleep patterns, and many people find them stressful.

—*Colleen Sullivan*

exclusively to their customers. As more homes became connected to cable, the industry came under greater regulation by local governments—oversight of rates and the prescribing of rules for what stations a cable operator could offer. During the 1990s, technological advances like fiber-optic cables led to significant increases in channel capacity, which was, in turn, used by an ever-growing number of cable networks, many of which (like CSPAN or CNN) carry specialized programming.

Water

Water utilities also provide an essential service to individuals and businesses, but unlike firms in other utilities, municipalities own the overwhelming majority of water utilities. They cover smaller geographic areas (typically a city or county). Furthermore, water utilities are typically responsible not only for providing water but also for processing wastewater and disposing of sewage. Many water utilities obtain their water from local reservoirs, but larger utilities (including those for New York City and Los Angeles) obtain water via aqueducts running from reservoirs hundreds of miles away. In some parts of the country, larger regional utilities sell water wholesale to local utilities. Water

companies are regulated by government agencies that establish water rates, access, and quality standards.

One of the most pressing issues facing municipal water utilities is maintaining adequate supplies of water to meet demand. Although periodic droughts naturally affect the availability of water, the more important concern is balancing the needs of residential and business customers. In California and Arizona competition between large commercial users of water, for example, farmers and residential developers, is intense.

Regulation of Utilities

All companies in the utilities industry are regulated by national, state, and local governments. Because utilities industries provide essential public services, this oversight is intended to ensure that these companies operate in the public interest. At the federal level, electric and gas companies are under the jurisdiction of the Federal Energy Regulatory Commission, which regulates the interstate transmission and sale of natural gas and electricity, oversees the licensing of hydroelectric projects, and administers the accounting and financial reporting of the companies it regulates. The Federal Communications Commission oversees telephone and cable companies; the Environmental Protection Agency establishes and supervises water quality standards for water utilities. Finally, the Securities and Exchange Commission has general oversight responsibility for any utility that issues securities to the public.

Extensive public utility regulation also occurs at state and local levels. Each state and most municipalities have public service commissions or boards whose members are either appointed or elected officials. One of the key responsibilities of state and local regulators is approving the rates charged utilities customers. The commissions also approve the construction of new facilities. State and local regulators, like the federal regulatory commissions, also act as a clearinghouse for consumer complaints.

Although most utilities were responsive to public needs, in the late twentieth century

A water pipeline, with electrical lines in the background, snakes through the desert in Owens Valley, California, 1983.

The Big 5
Energy Generators' Profits
(Millions of $)

Average increase in profits: 508%

Duke — up 374%
Dynegy — up 251%
Mirant (Southern) — up 36%
Reliant — up 1685%
Williams — up 195%

NOTES: Figures shown for Duke reflect energy services earnings before interest and taxes; for Dynegy, marketing and trading, recurring net income; for Mirant, earnings from operations; for Reliant, wholesale energy operating income; and for Williams, energy services profit. Source: Company Press Releases and Websites

Lt. Gov. Cruz Bustamante of California, left, confers with Assemblyman Dennis Cardoza, right, during a 2001 press conference where Cardoza outlined his legislation that would make overcharging for electricity a felony. The chart illustrates energy company profits before and after deregulation.

instances of unfair pricing, poor service, and general complacency caused federal officials to reexamine the monopoly status enjoyed by most utilities. One of the most significant acts to increase competition was the breakup of AT&T in 1984. As part of the settlement of a 1974 federal antitrust suit, the telephone giant agreed to divest itself of the 22 local telephone companies it owned in exchange for the right to enter new businesses. Federal regulators have since allowed a host of new companies to enter the long-distance and local telephone market. Congress has also enacted laws requiring deregulation of the utility industry. Legislation passed in 1978 partly deregulated natural gas prices and access to distribution systems; cable television was deregulated in 1984. In the 1990s state regulators began to end the monopoly status of gas and electric utilities by permitting business and residential consumers to select a supplier based on rates and service

Although increased competition and choice for consumers are cited as major reasons for deregulating public utilities, these companies still were required to provide these essential services reliably and at a fair cost. A number of unintended and unforeseen problems resulted. In the telephone industry, deregulation has led to lower rates and greater consumer options; however, new problems, including deceptive pricing and unethical practices like "slamming" (switching a customer's long-distance provider without consent) have emerged. Electric and gas customers have seen rates rise sharply during periods of high demand or low supply and in some cases experienced disruptions in service. In 2000 and 2001 parts of California experienced an energy crisis and intermittent blackouts caused, at least in part, by the way in which the state had deregulated the industry. Given such difficulties, the issue of how much government should regulate public utilities remains an open question.

Further Reading

Chambers, Ann. *Natural Gas and Electric Power in Nontechnical Language.* Tulsa, Okla.: PennWell, 1999.

Melosi, Martin V. *The Sanitary City: Urban Infrastructure in America from Colonial Times to the Present.* Baltimore, Md.: Johns Hopkins University Press, 2000.

Philipson, Lorrin, and H. Lee Willis. *Understanding Electric Utilities and De-regulation.* New York: M. Dekker, 1999.

Rudolph, Richard, and Scott Ridley. *Power Struggle: The Hundred-Year War over Electricity.* New York: Harper & Row, 1986.

Vietor, H. K. *Contrived Competition: Regulation and Deregulation in America.* Cambridge, Mass.: Belknap Press of Harvard University Press, 1994.

—David Mason

See also:
Assets and Liabilities;
Investment; Savings and
Investment Options; Scarcity;
Supply and Demand.

Valuation

Valuation is the process of estimating an asset's relative worth. Owning part or all of an asset, a business, or parcel of real estate, for example, is known as owning an interest in the asset. Ownership interests in companies and real estate are two kinds of assets that are commonly valued by estimating the monetary worth of interests at a specific time. Valuations of interests in businesses and real estate differ in many respects, and the methods used to value an asset in one kind of valuation may not be appropriate for another asset. Value is an estimated price at a given time under a particular definition of value.

Generally speaking, an asset's value depends on its scarcity (supply) and desirability (demand) among buyers and sellers at a particular time. To have monetary value, something must be concurrently both scarce and desirable. If something is highly desirable but not scarce, such as the air we breathe, people will not pay money for it. Assets like real estate or shares of a company's stock, on the other hand, tend to have monetary value because they are both desirable and scarce.

Valuers use different definitions of value depending on a valuation's purpose. The definition of value applied can greatly affect a valuation's results. Many business valuations are based on fair market value, and many real estate valuations use definitions of value that are similar to fair market value. The Internal Revenue Service, in its influential Revenue Ruling 59-60, has defined fair market value as: the price at which property would change hands between a willing buyer

and a willing seller when the former is not under any compulsion to buy and the latter is not under any compulsion to sell, both parties having reasonable knowledge of relevant facts.

Fair market value assumes the willingness and ability of both a buyer and seller to complete the transaction with payment in cash. Rather than showing value to a particular owner, the concept of fair market value is objective and seeks to find the price at which a reasonable investor would be willing to buy or sell.

Not all valuations, however, use fair market value or similar definitions of value. For example, valuations can be done from the perspective of a particular buyer or seller. Such valuations would probably not use the fair market value definition.

Public markets exist for the trading of certain standardized assets like agricultural products or stock in publicly traded companies. The New York Stock Exchange (for registered companies' securities and other commodities) is an example of a public market. Prices set in public markets reflect supply and demand for the assets traded at specified times and quantities. Public markets can provide useful pricing information to assist in the valuation of the traded assets and assets similar to them.

Many assets, however, have no public markets, and one or more valuation approaches must be used to estimate value. Many ways are available to value interests in privately held companies or real estate; the particular circumstances of each valuation will help determine which approaches and methods are most appropriate. Three valuation approaches are often considered when valuing interests in businesses or real estate. In many valuations, one or more of these approaches will not be useful, and valuers must exercise judgment in choosing and applying them. The three general approaches to valuation are the market-based approach, the asset-based approach, and the income-based approach.

The market-based approach estimates an asset's value by comparing it with similar

---

Formulas

Valuation
Value = scarcity (supply) + desirability (demand) at specific time

Valuation of Partial Interest
Value = Fair market value − minority interest − marketability discount

assets that have been bought or sold in the marketplace. This approach is based on the principle of substitution: a reasonable buyer would pay no more for one asset than it would cost to acquire an asset of equal utility.

The asset-based approach to value is also based on the principle of substitution: an asset's value is reflected in what it would cost to acquire an equivalent substitute. Using this approach in business valuation, all of a company's assets (both tangible and intangible) and liabilities are adjusted to current market values, with the difference between adjusted assets and adjusted liabilities representing the company's value to stockholders.

The income-based approach to value is based on the premise that an asset's value is equal to the present value of expected future benefits to the asset's owner. This valuation approach is usually performed by converting anticipated future benefits from owning the asset, for example, expected cash flows, into a present value, using an appropriate conversion rate. Rates used to convert future cash flows to a present value should reflect the risks associated with receiving the expected future cash flows, the owner's alternative investment opportunities, and the time value of money. The time value of money refers to an investor's preference for receiving money today rather than in the future.

Valuations of partial interests in companies or real estate can differ from valuations of entire companies or real estate parcels. In business valuation, a minority interest is ownership of less than 50 percent of the voting interest in a business. The fair market value of a minority ownership interest in a privately held company (or, for another example, a partial interest in real estate) may be worth significantly less than the interest's proportionate ownership interest in the entire company or real estate parcel. To reflect this, discounts are often applied to the whole company's value to determine the fair market value of a minority interest. In business valuation, a discount for lack of control, commonly

| **Approaches to Valuation** | |
Approach	Basis
Market-based	value compared to similar assets
Asset-based	value reflected in what it would cost to acquire an equivalent substitute
Income-based	value equal to present value of expected future benefits

known as a minority discount, may be applied to adjust for a minority interest's lack of control over company management, and a marketability discount may be applied to adjust for the difficulty in quickly selling an interest in a privately held company.

Marketability discounts are based on the difficulty of quickly selling interests that are not actively traded in public markets. Selling a minority interest in a privately held company is much more difficult than selling a minority interest in a publicly traded company, where investors can usually sell their stock and receive the cash in three business days. Accordingly, an investor is usually willing to buy a minority interest in a privately held company only at a discount compared with the price he or she would pay for the same percentage interest in an identical but publicly traded company.

Valuation is based on the likely perceptions and actions of a market using a particular definition of value and time appropriate for the valuation's purpose. Fair market value reflects the concept that an asset is worth the amount of money a willing buyer and seller would agree upon in light of alternative investment opportunities.

Further Reading
Damodaran, Aswath. *Investment Valuation: Tools and Techniques for Determining the Value of Any Asset.* 2nd ed. New York: John Wiley & Sons, 2002.
International Valuation Standards Committee. *International Valuation Standards 2001.* London: IVSC, 2001.

—*John D. Emory, Jr.*

Vanderbilt, Cornelius

1794–1877
Industrialist

Cornelius Vanderbilt played a prominent role in the U.S. steamship and railroad industries in the nineteenth century. Vanderbilt was fiercely competitive, and his ventures were characterized by a potent combination of frugal business operations and boundless persistence.

Vanderbilt was born to a poor family in Staten Island, New York, in 1794. He quit school at age 11 to work with his father, a farmer who sold produce to markets in New York City. When Vanderbilt was 16, he convinced his mother to lend him $100 after he helped to plant a small field. This $100 began Vanderbilt's long career in the steamship industry.

Vanderbilt used the money to start a ferry service between New York City and Staten Island in 1810. He charged customers 18 cents per trip, and he made more than $1,000 in his first year of business. (He

also repaid the loan to his mother.) During the War of 1812, Vanderbilt received a government contract to provide supplies to forts around New York; this contract allowed him to expand his collection of vessels. At that point, Vanderbilt earned the nickname "Commodore" for being in command of the largest schooner on the Hudson River. The nickname stuck with Vanderbilt throughout his life.

In 1818 Vanderbilt abandoned the ferry business, sold his boats, and turned to steamships, which were then being used to transport materials and people between New York City and Philadelphia. He worked as a ship's captain for Thomas Gibbons, who operated a service between New Brunswick, New Jersey, and New York City. Vanderbilt charged his customers $1.00, while other captains charged $4.00. He made up for low revenues from ticket sales by charging high prices for drinks at the ship's bar.

Vanderbilt left his position with Gibbons in 1829 and started his own ferry service between New York City and Peekskill, New York. He forced the competition out by cutting his rates to as low as 12.5 cents per trip. He later offered service between Albany, New York, and New York City, succeeding again by cutting rates. His business was so successful, in fact, that his competitors paid him to move it.

By the 1840s Vanderbilt was operating more than 100 steamships that sailed from New York City to a variety of destinations including Long Island Sound, Boston, Massachusetts, and Providence, Rhode Island. He employed more people than any other steamship company in the country, and his ships were known for their comfort. In 1846 Vanderbilt became a millionaire. Also in that year he developed his finest vessel to date, which he named the *Vanderbilt*; he later donated the ship to the U.S. government for use during the Civil War.

When the California Gold Rush began in 1849, Vanderbilt founded the Accessory Transit Company, which offered transport by steamship and overland from the East Coast to California. Vanderbilt's route went through

An engraving of Cornelius Vanderbilt, circa 1850s.

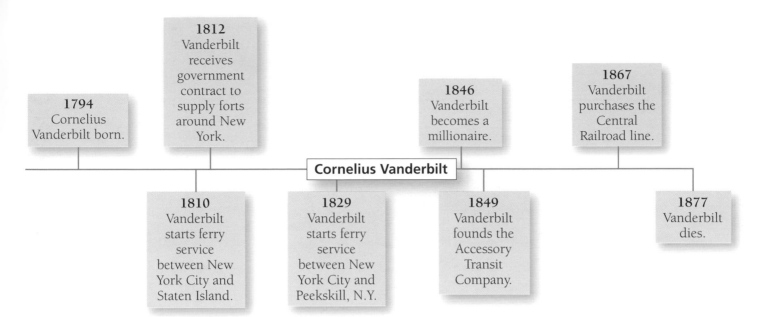

1794
Cornelius Vanderbilt born.

1812
Vanderbilt receives government contract to supply forts around New York.

1846
Vanderbilt becomes a millionaire.

1867
Vanderbilt purchases the Central Railroad line.

Cornelius Vanderbilt

1810
Vanderbilt starts ferry service between New York City and Staten Island.

1829
Vanderbilt starts ferry service between New York City and Peekskill, N.Y.

1849
Vanderbilt founds the Accessory Transit Company.

1877
Vanderbilt dies.

Nicaragua, while most other companies sent people through Panama. The itinerary cut 600 miles from the routes offered by others. Again, Vanderbilt cut prices for the trip in half, and again, he was ultimately paid by his competitors to get out of the business. Vanderbilt also started a passenger service between New York and France, but he sold the line at the beginning of the U.S. Civil War.

At age 70 Vanderbilt entered the railroad business, purchasing the New York, Harlem, and Hudson River rail lines. In 1867 he purchased the Central Railroad line, which allowed him to merge and improve rail services. In 1867 Vanderbilt tried to acquire the Erie Railroad; he failed, however, and lost a few million dollars in the attempt. Nonetheless, he eventually

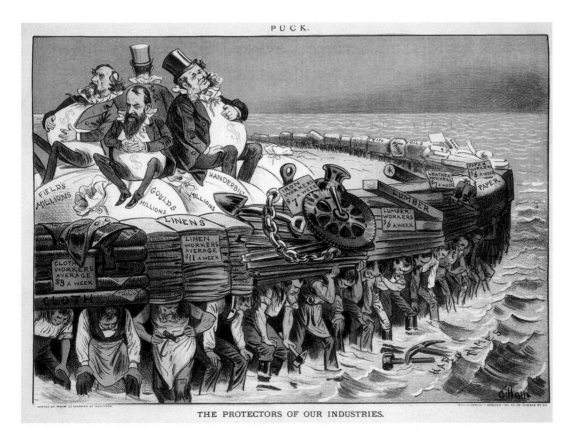

An 1883 cartoon shows Cornelius Vanderbilt and fellow millionaires riding on a raft of moneybags carried by workers of various professions.

A statue of Cornelius Vanderbilt on the campus of Vanderbilt University in Tennessee. The university was founded with a $1 million endowment from Vanderbilt in 1873.

extended his line to Chicago by acquiring the Lake Shore and Michigan Southern railroads, plus the Canadian Southern and the Michigan Central. Vanderbilt also played a pivotal role in creating Grand Central Terminal in New York City. He employed thousands of people during the Panic of 1873 to complete the project, which was crucial to the important New York–Chicago rail route.

After a long career that transformed the shipping and railroad industries, Vanderbilt died in 1877. Having started with an investment of $100, Vanderbilt ended as the richest man in the United States, with a net worth of about $95 million. During his lifetime he donated $1 million to Central University in Nashville, Tennessee, which later became Vanderbilt University.

Further Reading

Gordon, John Steele. *The Scarlet Woman of Wall Street: Jay Gould, Jim Fisk, Cornelius Vanderbilt, the Erie Railway Wars and the Birth of Wall Street.* New York: Weidenfeld & Nicolson, 1988.
Rodengen, J. *Legend of Cornelius Vanderbilt Whitney.* New York: Write Stuff Syndicate, 2000.

—*Karen Ayres*

Veblen, Thorstein

1857–1929
Economist

The economist and social theorist Thorstein Veblen was an eccentric and generally unpopular person. He questioned some of the basic orthodoxies of nineteenth-century economic theory and, in so doing, generated ideas that continue to be influential in the social sciences today.

Thorstein Bunde Veblen was born in Cato, Wisconsin, to Norwegian immigrant parents. He was educated first at Carleton College in Minnesota and subsequently at Johns Hopkins, Yale (where he obtained his doctorate in 1884), and Cornell. His first teaching post was at the University of Chicago, where he established his international reputation; he was later to teach at Stanford in California, the University of Missouri, and the New School for Social Research in New York City.

Classical economic theory at that time rested on two core assumptions. First, consumers were understood as rational individuals who generated economic demand by seeking the satisfaction of their own personal wants in the marketplace; in turn, producers served their own equally rational and individual interests by satisfying this demand, and the process of economic development was explained in terms of the coming together of supply and demand. Second, classical theory held that the market brought not only producers and consumers but also employers and workers into a mutually beneficial relationship: employers provided the capital, which created work opportunities for the employees.

The Theory of the Leisure Class (1899), Veblen's most famous and enduring work, challenged both these assumptions. Veblen observed that real-world economic decisions did not conform to the rationalism of the classical model, and that actual consumer preferences were difficult to explain in terms of conventional ideas of utility.

Why, for example, would someone economize on a basic need, such as food, to buy something decorative, like jewelry? Veblen sought answers in the other social sciences. Drawing on the research of anthropologists Lewis Morgan and Franz Boas, he argued that consumers are profoundly influenced in their decisions by the behavior of others around them. In assessing the utility of a product, an individual will take into account how others have assessed that utility. Therefore, Veblen argued, the autonomous consumer portrayed by economists like Adam Smith is a fiction.

Half a century earlier, Karl Marx and Friedrich Engels had challenged the assertion that the capitalist system worked to the mutual advantage of both workers and their employers. Marxism analyzed capitalist society in terms of the exploitation of a working class by a capitalist class. Veblen wrote in similar terms about an "industrious" class and a predatory "leisure" class that lived off the toil of others. However, he criticized the Marxists for their prediction of revolt by the

See also:
Consumerism; Galbraith,
John Kenneth; Marx, Karl;
Smith, Adam.

Social scientist Thorstein Veblen in an undated photograph.

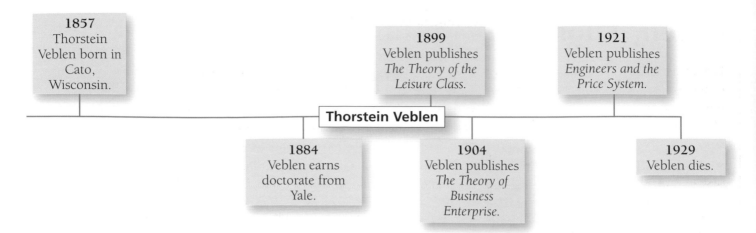

1857
Thorstein Veblen born in Cato, Wisconsin.

1899
Veblen publishes *The Theory of the Leisure Class.*

1921
Veblen publishes *Engineers and the Price System.*

Thorstein Veblen

1884
Veblen earns doctorate from Yale.

1904
Veblen publishes *The Theory of Business Enterprise.*

1929
Veblen dies.

working class and for their failure to explain the social stability that characterized actual capitalist societies. In contrast to Marx, Veblen interpreted the relationship between the industrious class and the leisure class in terms not of exploitation but of emulation: the industrious class admires the ability of the leisure class to acquire wealth without work and endeavors to emulate its behavior as far as possible.

The leisure class was defined by two emblems of social status, which Veblen termed "conspicuous leisure," a demonstrated nonreliance on work, and "conspicuous consumption," ostentatious expenditure on luxury goods. Veblen's analysis is more anthropological and psychological than economic: purchasing decisions that appear irrational in economic terms become rational in terms of how the consumer wishes to be perceived by others.

In *The Theory of Business Enterprise* (1904), Veblen argued that the concepts of emulation and conspicuous consumption combined to distort the operation of the capitalist system so that it ceased to resemble the model described by its eighteenth- and nineteenth-century apologists. The leisure class of capitalists, motivated exclusively by the pursuit of profit, would identify the business opportunities afforded by conspicuous consumption. Over time, this would increasingly divert society's productive energies from genuinely useful items and toward the frivolous.

Employers, workers, and consumers were all complicit in the cult of conspicuous consumption; engineers, by contrast, remained preoccupied with the solution of practical problems. Furthermore, with continued industrial development, the importance of the engineers to the production process would inevitably increase. This led Veblen, in *Engineers and the Price System* (1921), to envision a revolt of engineers and technicians against the degeneration of economic activity at the hands of profit-seeking businessmen. Although he did not

---

Key Ideas of Thorstein Veblen

- Capitalist society is divided into an "industrious" class and a predatory "leisure" class that lives off the toil of others.
- The leisure class is defined by "conspicuous leisure" and "conspicuous consumption."
- The industrious class endeavors to emulate the behavior of the leisure class.
- Emulation and conspicuous consumption combine to distort the operation of the capital system, diverting production from useful items toward the frivolous.
- With continued industrial development the importance of engineers will increase.
- Engineers and technicians will revolt against the degeneration of economic activity and emerge as the directors of society.

It has already been remarked that the term "leisure," as here used, does not connote indolence or quiescence. What it connotes is non-productive consumption of time. Time is consumed non-productively (1) from a sense of the unworthiness of productive work, and (2) as an evidence of pecuniary ability to afford a life of idleness. But the whole of the life of the gentleman of leisure is not spent before the eyes of the spectators who are to be impressed with that spectacle of honorific leisure which in the ideal scheme makes up his life. For some part of the time his life is perforce withdrawn from the public eye, and of this portion which is spent in private the gentleman of leisure should, for the sake of his good name, be able to give a convincing account. He should find some means of putting in evidence the leisure that is not spent in the sight of the spectators. This can be done only indirectly, through the exhibition of some tangible, lasting results of the leisure so spent—in a manner analogous to the familiar exhibition of tangible, lasting products of the labour performed for the gentleman of leisure by handicraftsmen and servants in his employ.

The lasting evidence of productive labour is its material product—commonly some article of consumption. In the case of exploit it is similarly possible and usual to procure some tangible result that may serve for exhibition in the way of trophy or booty. . . .

As seen from the economic point of view, leisure, considered as an employment, is closely allied in kind with the life of exploit; and the achievements which characterize a life of leisure, and which remain as its decorous criteria, have much in common with the trophies of exploit. But leisure in the narrower sense, as distinct from exploit and from any ostensibly productive employment of effort on objects which are of no intrinsic use, does not commonly leave a material product. The criteria of a past performance of leisure therefore commonly take the form of "immaterial" goods. Such immaterial evidences of past leisure are quasi-scholarly or quasi-artistic accomplishments and a knowledge of processes and incidents which do not conduce directly to the furtherance of human life. So, for instance, in our time there is the knowledge of the dead languages and the occult sciences; of correct spelling; of syntax and prosody; of the various forms of domestic music and other household art; of the latest properties of dress, furniture, and equipage; of games, sports, and fancy-bred animals, such as dogs and race-horses. In all these branches of knowledge the initial motive from which their acquisition proceeded at the outset, and through which they first came into vogue, may have been something quite different from the wish to show that one's time had not been spent in industrial employment; but unless these accomplishments had approved themselves as serviceable evidence of an unproductive expenditure of time, they would not have survived and held their place as conventional accomplishments of the leisure class.

develop his concept in any detail, he posited the evolution of a kind of technocracy, in which the engineers would emerge as the directors of society.

Veblen's importance in the history of economic thought lies in the connections he made between economics and other social sciences, especially anthropology and sociology. Many of his ideas continue to be important in contemporary economic and social analysis. "Conspicuous consumption" has entered the language, and Veblen's ideas underlie such common phrases as "keeping up with the Joneses." Veblen is often credited with having initiated the study of consumer trends, and his ideas have been used to explain seemingly bizarre marketing phenomena like pet rocks and brands of children's dolls. His ideas have also formed the basis of economic and cultural critiques of consumerism, including *The Affluent Society* (1958) by the economist John Kenneth Galbraith, who drew on Veblen to protest against "private affluence" in the midst of "public squalor."

Further Reading

Diggins, John Patrick. *Thorstein Veblen: Theorist of the Leisure Class*. Princeton, N.J.: Princeton University Press, 1999.
Jorgensen, Elizabeth Watkins. *Thorstein Veblen: Victorian Firebrand*. Armonk, N.Y.: M. E. Sharpe, 1999.
Veblen, Thorstein. *The Theory of the Leisure Class*. 1899. Reprint, New York: Dover, 1994.

—Peter C. Grosvenor

Venture Capital

For a business to expand, business owners need money. Usually the amount of money needed is much larger than the business owner alone can provide. Public companies can sell stock, but for a private company, especially a small private company, finding investors can be difficult. Small business owners can borrow money from friends and family, take out bank loans, vie for any available government grants. Although enough money might come from those sources to sustain a business or fund a small expansion, it is usually not enough to fund aggressive growth. Venture capital fills this need.

Kinds of Venture Capital

In its most general sense, venture capital is money and resources provided by investors to small businesses that wish to become large businesses. Providing venture capital is a high-risk game—very few small businesses actually become large ones. However, venture capital's impact on the economy at large is substantial because it enables entrepreneurs with new ideas and new technology to turn those ideas into substantial businesses.

In a sense, what is now called venture capital is very old. Throughout history wealthy people and institutions have funded entrepreneurs in hopes that their ideas would turn into successful businesses.

These days individuals who give money to new businesses are called angel investors; they invest in a new business in exchange for an ownership stake in the company. An angel investor is usually a seasoned businessperson who also provides advice, expertise, and useful business contacts. Angel investors tend to focus on start-up businesses or businesses that are very small—generally those that could use more management expertise and do not require huge amounts of capital.

Some large corporations, especially in the high-tech field, will fund start-ups they believe may produce products that could be useful to their core product. Intel, for example, which makes computer microprocessors, has funded start-ups developing technology that could make microprocessors faster. Such corporations also have in-house research and development departments, but start-ups are generally more likely to have innovative ideas and to take bigger risks in developing technology. Corporations sometimes take ownership stakes in the start-ups in return for the funding they give, but generally speaking, corporations are more interested in obtaining exclusive access to the new product once it is developed.

Businesses that are just starting out can also obtain assistance from incubators. Like an angel investor, an incubator provides more than just money—in fact, nonprofit incubators sometimes provide no cash at all. Instead, incubators provide facilities like

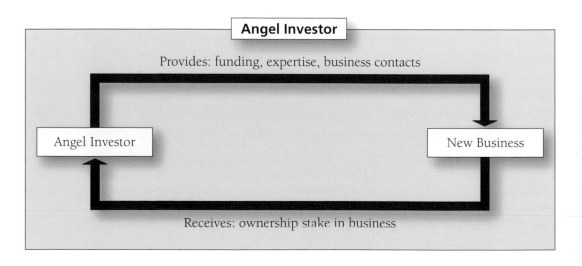

Angel Investor

Provides: funding, expertise, business contacts

Angel Investor → New Business

Receives: ownership stake in business

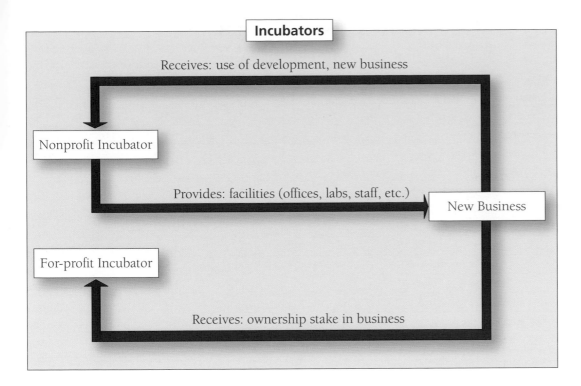

Incubators

Receives: use of development, new business

Nonprofit Incubator

Provides: facilities (offices, labs, staff, etc.)

New Business

For-profit Incubator

Receives: ownership stake in business

offices, high-speed Internet access, and support staff at little or no cost. Incubators can be run as a for-profit business, in which case the start-up provides the incubator with an ownership stake in return for use of the facilities. Many incubators are not-for-profit and are run by universities or municipal governments, which may also give tax breaks to the businesses in the incubators. With nonprofit incubators, start-ups do not always give an ownership share. Instead, a business might agree to let a university use any technology it develops free of charge. A municipality might not get anything at all in return for use of its incubator—except a slew of new businesses that are more likely to locate in the area once they are established enough to leave the incubator.

Probably the best-known providers of venture capital are venture capital firms—indeed, when people talk of the venture capital industry, they are usually referring to the firms, not angel investors or incubators. Venture capital firms run venture capital funds, which are generally set up as limited partnerships. The venture capital firm (or firms, as it is not uncommon for firms to join forces) is the general partner (the firm actually manages the fund and has also invested money into the fund). The limited partners,

who are the investors, provide the fund with money (usually a good deal of money—investing in a venture capital fund is beyond the means of most) and expect returns. In addition to providing money, the firm behind the fund offers management expertise and connections to other financiers and companies. A venture capital fund has a given lifespan, usually five to seven years. At the end of that period, the firm and the investors take their profits or losses, and the fund is disbanded.

Unlike angel investors, venture capital firms are a relatively new phenomenon. American Research and Development, a now-defunct Boston company established in 1946, is generally considered to have been the first venture capital firm. For decades, the industry was very small and clubby, and such firms generally dealt only with extremely wealthy families and institutions. Boston remains a center for the venture capital industry, but what is now known as Silicon Valley in California began to grow prominent in the industry in the 1960s. At the time, companies were beginning to develop expensive high-technology products, but most of the traditional financing firms were located on the East Coast, so West Coast financiers began to form venture

Venture Capital Commitments by Source 1995 to 2000 (in billion dollars)						
Source of funds	1995	1996	1997	1998	1999	2000
Capital commitments	9.9	11.8	17.1	29.4	60.0	92.9
Corporations	0.5	2.3	4.3	3.5	8.5	3.4
Endowments and foundations	2.0	1.4	2.8	1.9	10.3	19.6
Individuals and families	1.7	0.8	2.1	3.3	5.8	11.0
Financial and insurance	2.0	0.4	1.1	3.1	9.3	21.7
Pension funds	3.8	6.9	6.8	17.7	26.1	37.3
Percent of total commitments						
Corporations	5	20	25	12	14	4
Endowments and foundations	20	12	17	6	17	21
Individuals and families	17	7	12	11	10	12
Financial and insurance	20	3	6	10	16	23
Pension funds	38	58	39	60	44	40

Note: Totals may not add up because of rounding.
Source: U.S. Bureau of the Census, *Statistical Abstracts of the United States,* 2001,
http://www.census.gov/prod/2002pubs/01statab/business.pdf (April 9, 2003).

capital firms to help raise money for local businesses. Backing successful technology companies like Intel and Apple helped raise the profile of Silicon Valley venture capitalists, as well as the venture capital industry as a whole. The majority of West Coast venture capital firms are located in northern California, and most money in venture capital funds flows to the high-tech companies located there.

In the 1960s and 1970s the federal government became more involved in the venture capital industry with the creation of small-business investment companies (SBICs). SBICs received loans from the U.S. Small Business Administration to match funds raised privately for investment in small businesses; many venture capital firms organized as SBICs to gain access to these loans. In 1978 changes to the law made investing in venture capital funds by pension funds easier. Accordingly, such institutions have replaced the government as the major source of money in venture capital funds.

Exit Strategies

Some venture capital funds specialize in start-ups, but generally speaking, a company must already be fairly well established to attract money from a venture capital fund because the fund has a limited life span. When its time is up, investors and venture capital firms want to be able to cash out and to have more money than they put in. Consequently professional venture capitalists are very focused on what is known as the exit strategy. The exit strategy is the way in which the small companies that the venture capitalists have invested in are going to generate lots of cash for the venture capital fund. This is also known as a liquidity event, because it turns all of the value in the small company into liquid assets, usually cash or stock in a publicly traded company.

One kind of liquidity event is the sale of a small, private company to a much larger company. Say a venture capital fund invests in a small software company that is making an exciting new product used on desktop computers. The fund's investment and advice helps turn the company into a medium-sized software company that attracts a lot of media attention. It also attracts the attention of the software giant Microsoft Corporation, which buys the privately held company with a combination of cash and Microsoft stock. Cash is already liquid, and as Microsoft is a public company, its stock can easily be sold, so the venture capitalists have achieved a liquidity event and can cash out.

Another kind of liquidity event is to turn the private company into a public company and hold an initial public offering (IPO) of that company's stock. An IPO also makes the value of the company liquid, as its stock can be readily sold. In addition, going public makes shares of the company available to many more investors. If those investors are excited about the company, they will bid up the stock price, permitting the venture capital fund to sell its shares at an even greater profit.

Generally speaking, a company needs to be fairly large to attract either a buyer or enough investor interest to hold an IPO. As most companies that venture capital funds invest in are small, and the fund must achieve a liquidity event in a fairly short time, venture capitalists invest in companies that they think can expand very quickly. A company that wants to offer a service only in a specific locality is of no interest to venture capitalists, no matter how profitable that business might be, because that company will never grow very big. A company that wants to offer the same service nationally, however, will be of much greater interest to venture capitalists because the national market is much larger and the company will be much bigger.

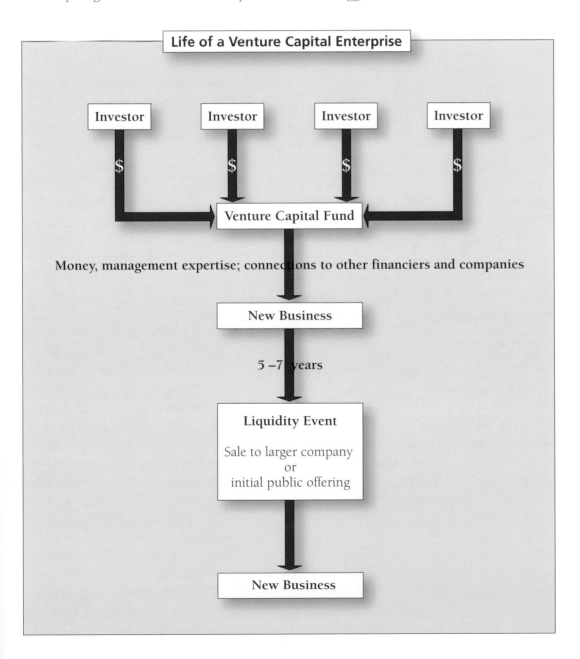

Life of a Venture Capital Enterprise

Investor → $ → Venture Capital Fund
Investor → $ → Venture Capital Fund
Investor → $ → Venture Capital Fund
Investor → $ → Venture Capital Fund

Money, management expertise; connections to other financiers and companies

New Business

5–7 years

Liquidity Event

Sale to larger company
or
initial public offering

New Business

Angus Davis, cofounder of Tellme Networks, Inc., poses in an English telephone booth at his company's offices in Palo Alto, California, in 1999. Davis announced that he and his partners at Tellme had received $47 million in funding from leading high-tech investors at rival venture capital firms. Unlike many venture capital–based companies founded in the late 1990s, in 2003 Tellme Networks remained in business.

This emphasis on expansion can lead to tremendous conflicts between the management of a small company and the venture capitalists who invest in it. A company's management may not want to expand as aggressively as the venture capitalists desire. Expanding aggressively may help the venture capitalists in the short run, but a company's management may believe that such a strategy will hurt the company in the long run. Because venture capitalists get an ownership stake in the company in return for their investment, they may be able to oust a company's existing management and replace it, which is rarely good for employee morale. On the other hand, as venture capitalists need the company to succeed to make money, they are often willing to dedicate a great deal of time, money, and effort to helping the company thrive. As a result, small companies that receive backing from venture capitalists are more likely to survive and grow than those that do not.

Boom and Bust

The majority of companies that venture capitalists invest in never make much money. A study of 1,765 investments in companies by venture capital funds from the mid-1980s to the mid-1990s found that fully 677 of the investments either lost money or broke even. Nonetheless, the amount of money invested overall increased tenfold because 89 companies returned more than 25 times the amount of money invested. The very small group of high-performance investments more than made up for the much larger group of bad investments.

The rule of thumb among venture capitalists is that only one of ten companies they invest in will really pay off. However, the payoff can more than compensate for the flops. Kleiner Perkins Caulfield & Byers, a venture capital firm, saw its investment in the online bookseller Amazon.com increase 6,000 percent. The investment of the three venture capital firms that backed the Internet-advertising company DoubleClick increased 9,930 percent. In 1997 the venture capital firm Benchmark Capital invested $5 million in the online auctioneer eBay for a share of the company that was worth $2.5 billion two years later—a return of 49,900 percent.

Such lavish returns are possible only if a liquidity event occurs, and that requires not just the right company but also the right business environment. Large corporations and small investors must be willing to buy the companies venture capital firms are selling. As a result, the venture capital industry is highly cyclical: when the economy is doing well, venture capital takes off; when the economy is doing poorly, venture capital crashes.

The most spectacular boom-and-bust to date began in the late 1990s; Internet companies like Amazon.com, DoubleClick, and eBay were red-hot, with investors gladly snapping up shares in IPOs. Many venture capital funds were generating very high returns, so investor money poured in and new funds and firms were established. In 1995 venture capital firms closed 1,899 funding deals with small companies; in 2000 they closed 8,151.

In April 2000 the market for Internet stocks crashed. The bust wiped out many publicly held Internet companies, but more important for venture capitalists, it made offering an IPO impossible—investors simply were not interested in putting their money into a crashing sector. For the rest of 2000 no Internet company was able to raise money through an IPO, cutting off what had become the major exit strategy for venture capitalists. Many firms shut down funds or went out of business altogether, and those that remained became much less willing to invest. In 2001 venture capital firms closed only 4,679 funding deals with small companies.

Although the bust certainly hurt the industry, many observers argue that in the long run a more conservative atmosphere will encourage venture capitalists to do what venture capital is supposed to do— fund worthwhile business ideas. Finding companies worth funding remains difficult but can generate tremendous rewards, both for the venture capitalists and for the economy as a whole.

Further Reading

Cardis, Joel, et al. *Venture Capital: The Definitive Guide for Entrepreneurs, Investors, and Practitioners*. New York: John Wiley & Sons, 2001.

Green, Milford B., ed. *Venture Capital: International Comparisons*. London: Routledge, 1991.

Harmon, Steve. *Zero Gravity 2.0: Launching Technology Companies in a Tougher Venture Capital World*. Princeton, N.J.: Bloomberg Press, 2001.

Southwick, Karen. *The Kingmakers: Venture Capital and the Money behind the Net*. New York: John Wiley & Sons, 2001.

Wright, Mike, and Ken Robbie, eds. *Venture Capital*. Adershot, U.K.: Dartmouth Publishing, 1997.

—*Mary Sisson*

Vocational Licensing

Vocational licensing involves the government determining who can engage in a particular profession. The practice arose because finding qualified workers can be a real challenge.

For example, a woman who knows nothing about construction wants to hire someone to put a new roof on her house. The job will pay well, so several people tell her that they are expert roofers. Some probably are, but some could be well-meaning incompetents or conniving frauds. As the woman knows nothing about how a roof should be built, how can she tell if the person she hires builds it correctly? Maybe the roof will look good to her untrained eye, but will it leak in rainstorms or fly off when the wind blows? She could rely on the recommendations of friends, but her friends do not necessarily know anything

about roofing either—perhaps the same dishonest roofer is swindling them all.

The homeowner is not the only one who will suffer. An honest and skilled roofer, for example, will suffer if people begin to suspect that most roofers are frauds. If the industry has a bad enough reputation, large numbers of people may even decide that they are better off going to the trouble of learning how to put on a roof themselves rather than exposing themselves to depredations of unscrupulous roofers. If no one hires roofers, then honest roofers will not be able to find work, and the entire roofing industry suffers.

Governments and industries have long tried to regulate the quality of skilled workers and service professionals. In the United States, state governments handle most licensing requirements. States began to demand that certain professionals obtain licensing in the eighteenth century, initially restricting licensing to doctors and lawyers—two professions that are hard for outsiders to

Replacing cedar shingles on a roof in 1996. Hiring licensed roofers helps assure homeowners that the work done will be of high quality.

understand and where the competency of individual practitioners is extremely important to public well-being.

Licensing eventually spread to many other professions. The eighteenth century also saw the beginnings of many professional associations that would later set their own rules for membership. The groups multiplied in the late nineteenth century as industrialization became widespread and more and more workers found themselves working with complex machinery that required special training to operate and fix. Worker safety was also a factor: the International Brotherhood of Electrical Workers established apprenticeship requirements in the late 1890s because inexperienced electricians were being killed on the job. By the early twentieth century such associations had started to lobby governments to accept similar rules as licensing requirements.

Higher education also became more widespread in the nineteenth century. Two-year postsecondary education, which provided specialized instruction for technical and skilled labor, was established in the early twentieth century. Such profession-specific education resulted in more and more workers performing specialized tasks that outsiders would have trouble evaluating. Because workers interested in particular professions were undergoing formal courses of instruction rather than informal apprenticeships, setting specific educational requirements for a license seemed reasonable.

By the 1950s the United States had some 1,200 vocational license laws on its books that covered 75 different professional categories. Doctors and lawyers are, of course, still required to get licenses, but so are many kinds of skilled workers, ranging from architects to embalmers to horseshoers.

Professional associations have generally encouraged the spread of licensing. Licensing benefits members of a particular profession in two ways: it helps secure a profession's reputation with the public, and it reduces competitive pressures on the profession as fewer people can enter it. Keeping out competitors tends to drive up the prices that those in the profession can

Requirements for Licensing as a Barber in Hawaii

PERSONAL REQUIREMENTS: Be at least 17 years of age.

PROFESSIONAL REQUIREMENTS: After qualifying for exam, a Temporary Permit is issued by completing a Temporary Permit application. The Temporary Permit is a privilege to work and train under supervision while waiting to take exams, and is valid for a period covering 4 exams (approximately 1 year). Temporary permit is issued only once and is not re-issued or extended. Applicants are encouraged to take the scheduled exams. Applicants with expired Temporary Permits who have not passed the exam are required to register as apprentices for 6 months before starting the licensing process again.

EXPERIENCE REQUIREMENTS: At least 1,500 clock hours of barber training. Experience will be recognized only after licensure and/or completion of training, and may be used to satisfy differences in training. Experience totaling not less than 6 months will be accepted.

Qualification may be satisfied by having an out-of-state license and may include verifying at least 6 months of experience since holding the license. The license is recognized only for the amount of training required for the license. If the training is less than 1,500 hours then a minimum of 6 months experience is necessary to satisfy any difference in the training requirement.

EXAMINATIONS: Written, multiple-choice exam tests the applicant's theoretical and practical knowledge in barbering and includes Hawaii Barber Law and Rules questions. Exams scheduled 4 times in one year, usually in March, June, September, and December at 5 test sites.

APPLICATION AND FEES: $20 for application, exam fee to be paid directly to testing agency, $25 for 2-year license, and $70 for biennial compliance resolution fund. Renewal fee every 2 years is $30. Temporary permit is $25.

—America's Career InfoNet, "Licensed Ocupations—Description," www.acinet.org (March 18, 2003)

charge, which is usually not a goal of the state governments that establish licensing processes. Nonetheless, higher prices for services can result from extending licensing requirements to a new profession. Such extensions are sometimes opposed by consumer groups for this reason; professional groups usually encourage licensing requirements.

Generally, states manage vocational licenses through licensing boards, which are usually made up of members of the profession being licensed. Licensing boards establish licensing requirements, which usually consist of a defined program of study combined with the passing of an exam. Licensing boards also often accredit schools that offer appropriate programs of study for people wishing to enter certain vocations. In addition, licensing boards may hear complaints by the public against licensed professionals and have the power to impose fines or even revoke licenses if the complaint is deemed justified.

In most cases if a person obtains a vocational license in one state, it is good in any state. Depending on the vocation, a state license may be required to practice or it may act as a seal of approval awarded to those who have undergone additional training. In the latter case, a person cannot claim to have a license she does not have, but she can still practice the profession. In the former case, she cannot practice the profession at all without the license—for example, practicing medicine without a license is a crime.

In recent years the rise of the technology industry has led to an increase in the popularity of certifications. Unlike a license, which is issued by a state, certifications are issued by the private sector, often by specific companies. For example, at least 500,000 people have received certification from Microsoft indicating that they have a particular level of expertise with one or more of its software products. Much like a state licensing board, Microsoft accredits classes and requires a candidate for certification to pass a proficiency exam.

Obviously, Microsoft's powers are not the same as a state's. Microsoft, for example, cannot prevent the uncertified from using its products. Certification has, however, become increasingly important to employers, who often require that job candidates for high-tech positions have specific certifications.

Although changes in education once influenced the popularity of licensing, the popularity of certification has had a profound impact on vocational and adult education. Many students now seek some form of certification in addition to or in place of a college degree. As a result, community colleges and vocational high schools have had to revise their offerings—an effort made more difficult by the fact that changes in the kinds of technology used lead to changes in the kinds of certification people want. In addition, private vocational schools that focus on offering certification have cropped up across the United States.

The increasing popularity of certification reflects a change in the economy—esoteric, specialized knowledge is more important now than ever. Despite the drawbacks of licensing, the growing need for workers with extremely specialized skills will probably make it more common in the years to come.

Some Occupations Requiring State Licenses

- Accountant, Certified Public
- Acupuncturist
- Architect
- Architect, Landscape
- Attorney
- Audiologist
- Barber
- Beautician
- Chiropractor
- Clinical Laboratory Technologist
- Commercial Fisher
- Contractor
- Dental Hygienist
- Dentist
- Detective, Private
- Electrician
- Embalmer
- Emergency Medical Technician
- Engineer
- Insurance Adjustor
- Massage Therapist
- Nuclear Medicine Technologist
- Nurse, Practical
- Nurse, Registered
- Optician
- Optometrist
- Pharmacist
- Physical Therapist
- Physician
- Plumber
- Podiatrist
- Psychologist
- Radiation Therapist
- Real Estate Broker
- Speech Pathologist
- Tattoo Artist
- Teacher
- Veterinarian

Further Reading

Berselli, Beth. "Voc-Ed Classes Aren't What They Used To Be: Now Hot and High-Tech, Trade Schools Go beyond Plumbing and Hairstyling." *Washington Post,* 26 March 1999, B9.

Cantor, Leonard. *Vocational Education and Training in the Developed World: A Comparative Study.* London: Routledge, 1989.

Evans, Rupert N., and Edwin L. Herr. *Foundations of Vocational Education.* 2nd ed. Columbus, Ohio: Merrill, 1978.

Smith, Doug. "From Motors to Modems: Vocational Education Classes Are Moving Away from an Emphasis on Manufacturing to Computer-Oriented Topics." *Los Angeles Times,* 21 January 1998, B2.

Swoboda, Frank. "Teaching Tomorrow's Work Force." *Washington Post,* 13 March 1994, H1.

Venn, Grant. *Man, Education and Work: Postsecondary Vocational and Technical Education.* Washington, D.C.: American Council on Education, 1964.

—*Mary Sisson*

Volkswagen

In German, the word *Volkswagen* means "people's car." The first Volkswagen, the Beetle, was designed to be just that.

Although German dictator Adolf Hitler could not drive, he was a car fanatic and an admirer of Henry Ford and his production lines; Hitler had read Ford's biography while in prison during 1923. At the 1934 Berlin auto show Hitler stated that his government would support the development of "a people's car." Hitler turned to automobile designer Ferdinand Porsche to create a car that could carry two adults and three children at a speed of 60 mph, get at least 33 miles to the gallon, and cost no more than 1,000 Reichmarks (around $140). Of the design, Hitler told Porsche, "It should look like a beetle, you've only got to look to nature to find out what streamlining is."

To save time and money, Porsche based the engine on a prototype he had designed a few years earlier. The resulting car, the Type 32, used an air-cooled, four-cylinder, horizontally opposed rear engine and featured beetle-like styling, some of which had been sketched out by Hitler. By late 1935 the first two prototypes, the V1 saloon and a convertible V2, were on the road. The development program was transferred to the Nazi German Labor Front, which used German worker contributions to pay for the construction of a new factory. Hitler also introduced a savings plan that would allow members of the public to purchase stamps that could be accumulated and used to pay for the car.

On May 26, 1938, Hitler laid the cornerstone of the new factory and declared that the first Volkswagen (VW) model would be known as the *Kraft durch Freude Wagen* (Strength through joy wagon). The town built to house the factory's workers was named *Stadt des KdF-Wagens* (Town of the strength-through-joy cars, later changed to Wolfsburg). The Kdf-Wagen could be bought only on a hire-purchase system, with the owner taking possession only when the final payment was made. By September 1, 1939, when the first cars were to start rolling off the production line, the Labor Front had received 336,668 orders. However, that day Hitler invaded Poland, and two days later France and Britain declared war. Although 640 Kdf-Wagens were built during World War II, these people's cars were all given away to Nazi Party officials. No one who had paid a deposit ever received a car.

During the war the Volkswagen factory built military vehicles using the same chassis and air-cooled engine developed for the Kdf-Wagen. Later, the factory used forced labor to repair aircraft and to build the V1 buzz bombs, unmanned airplanes used to shell London. Allied air raids left the factory largely in ruins.

See also:
Advertising Industry; Ford, Henry; Transportation Industry.

Volkswagen

1923
Adolf Hitler reads Henry Ford's biography while in prison.

1938
Hitler lays cornerstone for first Volkswagen factory.

1949
Volkswagen exports Beetles to United States.

1960
Volkswagen hires advertising agency Doyle Dane Bernbach.

1972
Beetle overtakes Ford Model T to become the best-selling car in history.

1978
Last Beetle produced in Germany.

1998
Revamped Beetle launched.

From Wartime to Modern Times

At the end of the war, the British had the responsibility for governing the Wolfsburg area. The British administrators decided that the Strength through joy car would make an excellent transport for the occupying forces. The car was renamed the Beetle, and production was begun using old stock and equipment that survived the bombing. The factory produced about 1,000 cars per month in 1946, including a two-seat convertible called the Radclyffe Roadster, after Charles Radclyffe, a British colonel.

In 1948, after the appointment of Heinz Nordhoff as the VW factory's general director, the go-ahead was given to produce a prototype convertible version of the Beetle—the Karmann. Although the Allied investigating committee felt the Beetle had no commercial potential (the Allies were still in charge of Germany's postwar industrial sector), Nordhoff believed the car could be successful. As early as 1949 Volkswagen began exporting Beetles to the United States. Nordhoff had correctly reasoned that the car's unique design, low price, and reliable construction would make it popular. The Volkswagen Karmann would become the best-selling convertible in the world.

Volkswagen generated many favorable stories in the American automotive press during the 1950s, including glowing reviews in *Consumer Reports*. By 1959 Volkswagen was the largest-selling imported car in America. That year Volkswagen sold 119,899

The first shipment of Volkswagens to the United States arriving in Baltimore, Maryland, in 1956.

cars, representing 20 percent of the total import car market.

One of the reasons for Volkswagen's success was the company's mischievous ads. Traditional car advertisements discussed straightforward qualities like size and comfort. In 1960 Volkswagen hired advertising agency Doyle Dane Bernbach to design a campaign that would use humor and self-deprecation to sell cars. Volkswagen ads, with tag lines like "Think small," "Lemon," and "Small, ugly, reliable," have become almost as famous as the car itself. The ads also appealed to the young people who became Volkswagen's largest customers during the 1960s. By poking fun at traditional advertising, VW tapped into a vein of hip cynicism with the status quo that was emerging in the 1960s. During that decade, Volkswagen became an icon of the counterculture.

On February 17, 1972, the Beetle overtook the Ford Model T to become the best-selling car in history. The last Beetle to be made in Germany left the production line in January 1978, but production continued in the company's Puebla, Mexico, factory, originally built in 1954. The 20,000,000th Beetle rolled off the Mexican production line in May 1981; with demand in Europe still high, Volkswagen of Germany was importing Beetles from Mexico until 1985.

Beginning in the 1980s, Volkswagen also began to acquire and redevelop automobile companies, including Audi, MAN, SEAT, Skoda, and Lamborghini. The company's ability to design cheap, reliable cars that appeal to young people has kept it financially strong, even during difficult times in the auto manufacturing industry. As the youth of the 1960s grew up, their taste in cars changed, and Volkswagen designed new cars to keep up with changing attitudes. In 1998 a revamped version of the Volkswagen Beetle hit the roads, reconceptualized as an expensive status symbol for baby boomers. Other models—the Volkswagen Van, Gulf, and Passat—have each become people's cars for different generations.

The redesigned Volkswagen Beetle unveiled at the North American International Auto Show in Detroit in 1998.

Further Reading
Nelson, Walter Henry. *Small Wonder: The Amazing Story of the Volkswagen.* Boston: Little, Brown, 1970.
Rosen, Michael J., ed. *Tales of the Car That Defined a Generation.* New York: Artisan, 1999.
Shuler, Terry. *Volkswagen: Then, Now, and Forever.* Indianapolis, Ind.: Beeman Jorgensen, 1997.

—*Lisa Magloff*

See also:
Civil Rights Legislation;
Innovation; Women in the
Workforce.

Walker, Madame C. J.

1867–1919
Hair and beauty entrepreneur

Sarah Breedlove McWilliams Walker (neé Sarah Breedlove) was one of the first American women to become a self-made millionaire. She was a child of freed slaves and had almost no formal education, making her story even more extraordinary.

Sarah Breedlove was born in 1867 to Minerva and Owen Breedlove. Her parents, both former slaves, were sharecroppers on a

Madame C. J. Walker, circa 1914.

plantation in northeast Louisiana. They had both died by the time Breedlove was seven, and from that time she supported herself, at first by working in the cotton fields. When she was 14, she married Moses McWilliams (changing her name to Sarah Breedlove McWilliams). She had a daughter Lelia (later changed to A'Lelia) in June 1885. When Sarah's husband died two years later, McWilliams moved to St. Louis, Missouri, to join her four brothers, who worked as barbers. For the next 18 years, from 1887 to 1905, she supported herself and her daughter by working as a washerwoman.

Hair Entrepreneur

During the 1890s McWilliams began to suffer from a scalp ailment that caused her to lose most of her hair. She began experimenting with home and commercial remedies to try to cure her condition and eventually began developing her own remedies and hair care products.

McWilliams sold her products door-to-door throughout St. Louis. She mixed up her soaps and ointments in washtubs, using kitchen utensils and developing curling tools and hairdressing techniques specifically for African Americans' hair. In 1905 McWilliams moved to Denver, Colorado, to join her widowed sister-in-law and nieces. Six months later she married newspaperman Charles Joseph Walker and changed her name to Walker, calling herself Madame C. J. Walker (She kept the name even after business differences ended the marriage.) That same year she established the Madame C. J. Walker Manufacturing Company.

The Madame C. J. Walker Manufacturing Company marketed a complete hair care and straightening system called the Walker Method. At that time most African American women wanted to straighten their hair. The most popular method was ironing—placing the hair on a flat surface and literally pressing it with a hot iron. However, this dehydrated the hair, leaving it brittle and lusterless. The Walker Method was to prove a very popular alternative; it used a shampoo, a pomade—Madame C. J. Walker's

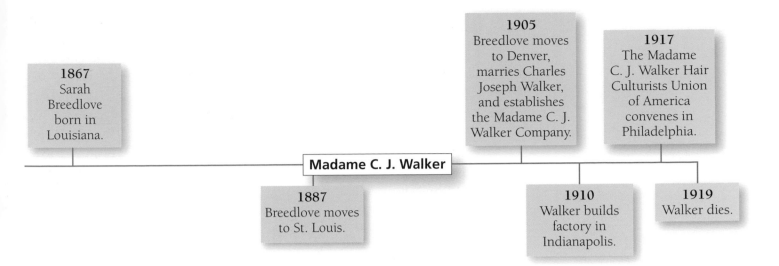

1867
Sarah Breedlove born in Louisiana.

1887
Breedlove moves to St. Louis.

1905
Breedlove moves to Denver, marries Charles Joseph Walker, and establishes the Madame C. J. Walker Company.

Madame C. J. Walker

1910
Walker builds factory in Indianapolis.

1917
The Madame C. J. Walker Hair Culturists Union of America convenes in Philadelphia.

1919
Walker dies.

Hair Grower—made from petrolatum and medicinal sulfur, and heated iron combs to straighten the hair.

The company used an army of agent-operators to sell Walker's treatments door-to-door. Known as Walker Agents, they became familiar figures throughout the United States and the Caribbean, where they made house calls, always dressed in white blouses tucked into long black skirts and carrying black satchels containing the ingredients of the Walker Method.

By early 1910 Walker had settled in Indianapolis, Indiana, then the nation's largest inland manufacturing center, where she built a factory, a hair and manicure salon, and a training school for hair culturists. Within three years the Madame C. J. Walker Manufacturing Company employed more than 3,000 African Americans, and Walker began traveling within Central America and the Caribbean to expand her business.

Lelia Walker moved to New York City in 1914 and built a $90,000 townhouse on West 136th Street. The residence was designed by the first registered black architect in New York, Vertner Woodson Tandy. (In the 1920s, Lelia Walker, then Mrs. A'Lelia Walker Robinson Wilson Kennedy, presided over a famous salon known as "The Dark Tower," where talented African American writers, musicians, and artists met with white intellectuals.) Madame Walker moved to New York in 1916 and built a country home at Irvington-on-Hudson, New York.

The $250,000 mansion was nicknamed Villa Lewaro (after the first syllables in her daughter's name—Lelia Walker Robinson) by tenor Enrico Caruso.

As her business continued to grow, Walker organized her agents into local and state clubs. Her Madame C. J. Walker Hair Culturists Union of America convention in Philadelphia in 1917 was one of the first national meetings of businesswomen in the country. Walker used the gathering not only to reward her agents for their business success, but to encourage political activism as well. "This is the greatest country under the sun," she told them at one meeting, "but we must not let our love of country, our patriotic loyalty cause us to abate one whit in our protest against wrong and injustice."

African American Icon
Although Walker continued to oversee her business and to run a New York office, she also quickly became involved in Harlem's burgeoning social and political life. She took special interest in the antilynching movement, contributing $5,000 to the National Association for the Advancement of Colored People (NAACP), the largest donation the 10-year-old organization had received to that time. In July 1917, when a white mob murdered more than three dozen blacks in East St. Louis, Illinois, Walker joined a group of Harlem leaders who visited the White House to present a petition demanding federal antilynching legislation.

A'Lelia Walker, daughter of Madame C. J. Walker, gets a manicure at one of her mother's beauty shops in New York City, circa 1920s.

Walker also encouraged her agents to support black philanthropic work, awarding prizes for the Walker Club that donated the most money to charity every year. She made the single largest donation to the National Association of Colored Women for their successful 1918 campaign to purchase the home of Frederick Douglass and preserve it as a museum. She funded scholarships for young women and men at Tuskegee Institute and contributed to Palmer Memorial Institute, a private secondary school for blacks in Sedalia, North Carolina.

Walker died on May 25, 1919, at Villa Lewaro. The company passed to her daughter and remained in the family until it went out of business in 1985. Much of the balance of Walker's estate was willed to the NAACP.

Because Walker's fortune was built on products like hair straightening formulas, which enabled black women to have hair more like their white counterparts, Walker has occasionally been considered problematic by contemporary scholars. However, when considered in their historical context, Walker's achievements were formidable. In her lifetime, Walker established herself as a pioneer of the modern black hair care and cosmetics industry and set standards in the African American community for corporate and community giving. She was one of the first self-made American businesswomen of any race.

Further Reading

Blashfield, Jean F. *Women Inventors*. Minneapolis, Minn.: Capstone Press, 1996.

Colman, Penny. *Madame C. J. Walker: Building a Business Empire*. Brookfield, Conn.: Millbrook Press, 1994.

Lommel, Cookie. *Madame C. J. Walker*. Los Angeles: Melrose Square Publishing, 1993.

—Lisa Magloff

Wall Street Journal

The *Wall Street Journal* is the leading business newspaper in the United States. Established in 1889, the *Journal's* daily circulation eventually reached into the millions, making it one of the most widely read newspapers in the world. Nicknamed the Republican Bible, the *Journal* is also an influential voice of political conservatism, advocating free markets and limited government.

The *Wall Street Journal* had its origins in the expanding economy of the post–Civil War period. A growing stock market fueled investor demand for up-to-date financial news. The Kiernan News Agency was an early pioneer in financial reporting. It distributed hand-delivered news bulletins to subscribers. In the 1870s Kiernan added a ticker service transmitting stock data via telegraph. These bulletins and ticker tapes conveyed stock prices, company earnings, and other market information. In 1882 two young reporters for the agency, Charles Dow and Eddie Jones, started a bulletin service of their own in New York City. They invited silent partner Charles Bergstresser to form Dow, Jones & Company, the future publisher of the *Wall Street Journal*.

The three founders contributed different talents to the upstart agency. Introverted, cerebral Dow wrote penetrating studies of the financial markets; his vision was to provide cogent analysis rather than just the facts and gossip circulated by other news agencies. Jones was an extroverted man-about-town who ingratiated himself with Wall Street investors and brokers. He was responsible for managing the messenger boys who ran bulletins to clients in Manhattan. Bergstresser invested a large amount of capital and had many important contacts on Wall Street, including banker J. Pierpont Morgan.

Dow Jones's future lay not with the bulletin services but with the afternoon newspaper it created in 1883. The one-page *Customers' Afternoon News Letter* summarized the day's bulletins and reported Wall Street gossip. Originally intended for stockbrokers, the *News Letter* found a wider audience among investors. Six years later the company expanded the letter into a full-fledged newspaper, the *Wall Street Journal*. The *Journal* published financial news and tables listing the closing prices of stocks and bonds. It also reported the price index of stocks making up the Dow Jones Industrial Average (DJIA), a representative collection of blue-chip securities. The DJIA eventually became a news item itself, a barometer of stock activity widely reported in daily newspapers, the radio, and television.

See also:
Dow Jones Averages; Great Depression; Publishing Industry; Stocks and Bonds.

Wall Street Journal

1882
Charles Dow, Eddie Jones, and Charles Bergstresser form Dow, Jones & Company.

1889
Dow Jones establishes the *Wall Street Journal*.

1912
Clarence Walker Barron takes over the *Wall Street Journal*.

1947
Wall Street Journal wins its first Pulitzer Prize.

1975
Wall Street Journal pioneers satellite transmission of typeset pages.

1996
Wall Street Journal launches on-line edition.

2001
Wall Street Journal staff forced to evacuate offices following September 11 terrorist attacks.

Clarence Walker Barron, publisher of the Wall Street Journal, *in 1925.*

Despite its parochial title, the *Journal* sought a national audience by reporting business news from across the country. The *Journal* had an agreement with newspaper magnate Clarence Walker Barron. *Journal* editors exchanged Wall Street news for reports from Barron's newspapers in Boston and Philadelphia. In 1897 the *Journal* established a bureau in Washington, D.C., to report on government. Dow wrote the popular Review and Outlook column educating general readers about the stock market. His editorials attacked Populist proposals to inflate the currency but cautioned bankers that they could not ignore public sentiment. The newspaper earned a reputation for fair-minded business conservatism. This combination of timely information from other cities, Dow's news commentary, and the paper's useful statistical data sent circulation soaring to 12,000 by 1903. Advertising revenue also increased as sellers of luxury items targeted the *Journal's* wealthy readers.

By 1902 Dow was seriously ill and could no longer manage the growing enterprise. He and Bergstresser sold their company shares to Clarence Walker (C.W.) Barron (Jones had resigned to join a brokerage firm). To protect his fortune from damaging libel judgments, Barron transferred his stock to his wife, Jessie, a then-common practice of newspaper publishers.

Mrs. Barron directed the company for the next 10 years until slipping circulation and advertising revenue prompted C.W. to take over the flagging *Journal* in 1912.

Barron was a bigger-than-life businessman and brilliant journalist who raised the *Wall Street Journal* to international prominence. During World War I he traveled to Europe and interviewed the world's most important financial leaders. Barron's series of articles on the Federal Reserve, wartime finance, and the oil industry became major books. He livened up the *Journal's* format by adding graphics and columns on humor, gossip, and Washington politics. By 1921 circulation had rebounded to 20,000, and, capitalizing on his fame, the *Journal* promoted a new financial weekly, *Barron's.*

The *Journal* and *Barron's* rode the boom of the 1920s, with circulation exceeding 50,000 by the end of the decade. Public fascination with the stock market turned a *Wall Street Journal* subscription into a status symbol. Publication of a separate Pacific Coast edition of the *Journal* boosted its claim to being a national newspaper. Thus, when C.W. Barron died in 1928, his newspaper seemed secure.

The stock market crash of 1929 and the Great Depression that followed greatly damaged the reputation of Wall Street. Circulation and advertising revenue plummeted. Editor Kenneth C. Hogate also faced a hostile political environment. During the previous decade, the *Journal* had defended business and the Republican Party from its critics. This honeymoon with the party in power ended as President Franklin D. Roosevelt, a Democrat, signed into law many new government programs. Although the *Journal* supported government regulation of the stock market, it denounced Roosevelt and the Democrats for their big spending and business bashing. In the late 1930s Sen. Harry Truman (D–Missouri) retorted that the newspaper had become "the Republican Bible."

During the New Deal era, the *Journal* became more concerned with politics and government. Washington bureau chief Barney

The scene on Wall Street in New York City on October 24, 1929, the day the stock market crash began.

Kilgore provided insightful explanations of the new laws affecting business. The *Wall Street Journal* also printed the entire text of presidential speeches and major pieces of legislation. Later, as Europe plunged into war, the *Journal* paid more attention to foreign policy. Although informative, this political news coverage failed to revive circulation, which by 1932 had tumbled to half its 1929 high and remained at that level throughout the decade.

The situation improved when Barney Kilgore took over as editor in 1942. During the next quarter-century, Kilgore revolutionized the *Journal* by broadening its appeal to consumers. He directed reporters to "hook" readers with eye-catching headlines and stories written in plain English. In 1947 the *Journal* won the first of many Pulitzer Prizes. By 1966, the year Kilgore retired, general circulation had reached one million. Its educational service also brought the *Journal* into thousands of high school and college classrooms. Politically, *Wall Street Journal* editors remained conservative on economic issues but supported the civil rights movement and opposed U.S. intervention in the Vietnam War.

Kilgore's successors further expanded the *Wall Street Journal*. In 1975 the newspaper pioneered satellite transmission of typeset, making the same edition available to subscribers nationwide. A two-section *Journal* appeared (1980) followed by a

Copies of the Wall Street Journal *are sold during morning rush hour in New York City.*

three-section paper (1988), thus making space available for coverage of new topics, including media, law, technology, and small business. Dow Jones also launched *Asian Wall Street Journal* and *Wall Street Journal Europe*. In 1996 the *Journal* went online with an Internet edition (www.wsj.com). Editor in chief Robert Bartley transformed the opinion–editorial page by establishing a board of contributors made up of distinguished writers in politics and economics. The op-ed page, always an outlet for conservative intellectuals, now attracted opposing viewpoints, making for lively debates.

Since the early 1980s the *Wall Street Journal* has faced new competition. *USA Today* imitated the *Journal's* satellite transmission, becoming the second U.S. newspaper to go national. Other publications, *Business Week* and *Forbes* among them, undercut the *Wall Street Journal* by offering volume discounts to major advertisers. As a result the *Journal's* circulation has slowly declined from its 1981 peak of two million. Nevertheless, it remains one of the highest-circulation newspapers in the country.

September 11, 2001, and the *Journal*

The terrorist attack of September 11, 2001, highlighted how important the *Wall Street Journal* is to the American businessperson's day. When two hijacked planes crashed into the World Trade Center towers, debris showered on *Journal* offices. Forced to evacuate by ferry, train, and car, *Wall Street Journal* staffers made it to the newspaper's remote office in South Brunswick, New Jersey.

Remarkably, a handful of reporters and editors got out the next day's edition. For only the second time in its history (the first being the Japanese attack on Pearl Harbor), the *Journal* ran a banner headline: Terrorists Destroy World Trade Center, Hit Pentagon in Raid with Hijacked Jets. In the days following the attack, grateful readers thanked the newspaper for carrying on in the midst of adversity and helping to restore calm to the business community.

Further Reading

Dealy, Francis X. *The Power and the Money: Inside the* Wall Street Journal. Secaucus, N.J.: Carol Publishing Group, 1993.

Rosenberg, Jerry Martin. *Inside the* Wall Street Journal: *The History and the Power of Dow Jones & Company and America's Most Influential Newspaper.* New York: Macmillan, 1982.

Scharff, Edward E. *Worldly Power: The Making of the* Wall Street Journal. New York: Beaufort Books, 1986.

Wendt, Lloyd. *The* Wall Street Journal: *The Story of Dow Jones & the Nation's Business Newspaper.* Chicago: Rand McNally, 1982.

—*Jonathan J. Bean*

Wal-Mart

Although discount chain stores like Wal-Mart now constitute a common and popular form of retailing in the United States, many people were suspicious of discount retailing when it first appeared in the 1950s. Traditional retailers and manufacturers resisted opening discount stores, primarily because they believed discounting would cause them to lose control of the marketplace. Until the early 1960s most states placed legal restrictions on discount retailing. As discount stores have caught on, however, they have changed the way people shop, the way people think about shopping, and the retail business generally.

Wal-Mart was not America's first discount chain, and for much of its early existence it was largely ignored by others in the retail industry. Wal-Mart Stores, Inc., is now the world's largest retailer, and many of the retailing concepts pioneered by founder Sam Walton and his Wal-Mart stores are standard practice throughout the industry.

In 1945, at the age of 27, Sam Walton opened his first variety store, a franchise of the Ben Franklin chain, in Newport, Arkansas. Six years later, Walton began opening his own variety stores under the name Walton's Five and Dime.

By the time discount retailing began to emerge in the early 1960s, Walton already owned 15 variety stores, located mostly in Arkansas, Missouri, and Oklahoma. These were traditional small-town stores with relatively high price markups. Walton, an ardent student of retailing theory, kept up with innovations in the industry. When a barber named Herb Gibson from Berryville, Arkansas, began opening discount stores outside towns where Walton ran variety stores, Walton was quick to anticipate the success of this new trend in retailing. Walton opened the first Wal-Mart store in Rogers, Arkansas, in 1962, the same year in which S. S. Kresge launched Kmart, F. W. Woolworth started Woolco, and Dayton Hudson began the Target chain.

From the beginning Walton was determined to offer the lowest prices in the discount retail industry. To achieve that goal, Walton had to lower his costs below those of other discount retailers. Accordingly, profit margins had to be cut to an absolute minimum; for the chain to stay in business with such low profit margins, sales volume had to grow relentlessly. Achieving steadily rising sales volume could be accomplished by opening new stores in new markets. Rather than open stores in large cities, where costs were high and competition from other discount chains was in place, Walton concentrated on rural areas. In many cases Wal-Mart was the first discount store to appear in these areas.

To select locations for expansion, Walton would fly low over the countryside in his

See also:
Just-in-Time Inventory;
Overhead; Retail and
Wholesale; Total Quality
Management.

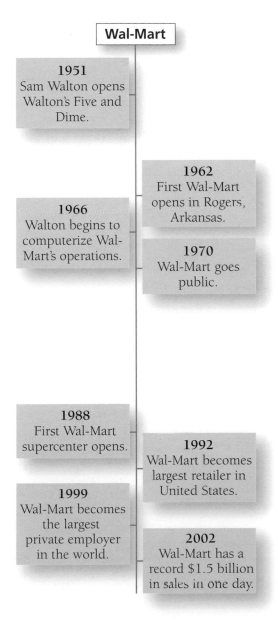

Wal-Mart

1951
Sam Walton opens Walton's Five and Dime.

1962
First Wal-Mart opens in Rogers, Arkansas.

1966
Walton begins to computerize Wal-Mart's operations.

1970
Wal-Mart goes public.

1988
First Wal-Mart supercenter opens.

1992
Wal-Mart becomes largest retailer in United States.

1999
Wal-Mart becomes the largest private employer in the world.

2002
Wal-Mart has a record $1.5 billion in sales in one day.

airplane, studying the layout of the small towns. When he found a spot he liked, he would touch down, buy a piece of farmland at that intersection, and begin plans to build another Wal-Mart store. Because the stores were built away from town centers and were all built using the same simple design, they could be constructed quickly and cheaply.

Walton pioneered many aspects of discount retailing that are now taken for granted. Very quickly Walton realized that computerized merchandise tracking was crucial to maintaining control of a large inventory. As early as 1966 with only 20 Wal-Mart stores, Walton began to computerize his operations. He visited colleges and hired computer engineering students on the spot to design Wal-Mart's inventory control systems. Today Wal-Mart's computer database is said to be second only to the Pentagon's in capacity. Early computerization allowed

---

Sam's Ten Rules for Building a Business

Rule 1 Commit to your business. Believe in it more than anybody else. . . . If you love your work, you'll be out there every day trying to do it the best you possibly can, and pretty soon everybody around will catch the passion from you—like a fever.

Rule 2 Share your profits with all your Associates, and treat them as partners. In turn, they will treat you as a partner, and together you will all perform beyond your wildest expectations. . . .

Rule 3 Motivate your partners. Money and ownership alone aren't enough. Constantly, day-by-day, think of new and more interesting ways to motivate and challenge your partners. . . .

Rule 4 Communicate everything you possibly can to your partners. The more they know, the more they'll understand. The more they understand, the more they'll care. Once they care, there's no stopping them. . . .

Rule 5 Appreciate everything your Associates do for the business. . . . Nothing else can quite substitute for a few well-chosen, well-timed, sincere words of praise. They're absolutely free—and worth a fortune.

Rule 6 Celebrate your successes. Find some humor in your failures. Don't take yourself so seriously. Loosen up, and everybody around you will loosen up. . . .

Rule 7 Listen to everyone in your company. And figure out ways to get them talking. The folks on the front lines—the ones who actually talk to the customer—are the only ones who really know what's going on out there. You'd better find out what they know. . . .

Rule 8 Exceed your customers' expectations. . . . The two most important words I ever wrote were on that first Wal-Mart sign, "Satisfaction Guaranteed." They're still up there, and they have made all the difference.

Rule 9 Control your expenses better than your competition. . . . You can make a lot of different mistakes and still recover if you run an efficient operation. Or you can be brilliant and still go out of business if you're too inefficient.

Rule 10 Swim upstream. Go the other way. Ignore the conventional wisdom. If everybody else is doing it one way, there's a good chance you can find your niche by going in exactly the opposite direction.

—Sam Walton, *Made in America*, 1992

Wal-Mart to develop just-in-time inventory control—ordering items from suppliers only when they were needed, not at fixed, predetermined times. This allowed Wal-Mart to keep a low inventory, which translated into low overhead costs.

These innovations in retailing paved the way for the emergence of other discount chains like Blockbuster and Barnes & Noble. Because these large chains offer attractive prices and convenient shopping, they often dominate the markets they enter, sometimes driving smaller competitors out of business. In fact, as Wal-Mart grew, this dynamic became a point of condemnation: critics complained that Wal-Mart littered the landscape with ugly warehouse stores and put small, local stores out of business. By locating stores on highways or large roads on the outskirts of towns, Wal-Mart and other discount retailers also tended to draw traffic and shoppers away from town centers while increasing traffic elsewhere. Many small towns therefore have resisted plans for new Wal-Marts and other discount retailers. Wal-Mart's expansions, of course, have been possible only because local consumers chose in large numbers to shop at Wal-Mart stores. Nonetheless, in response to criticisms, Wal-Mart has developed a new chain of smaller, more attractively designed stores called Neighborhood Markets.

Selling to the World

In 1970, when Wal-Mart had 30 stores in Arkansas, Missouri, and Oklahoma, the company went public (offered shares of its stock for sale to the public) to raise capital to speed the pace of its expansion. In 1979 Wal-Mart had its first billion-dollar sales year. By 1992, when Wal-Mart overtook Sears Roebuck to become the nation's largest retailer, 1,720 Wal-Mart stores were in operation; in the following year the company had its first billion-dollar sales week. By 2000 Wal-Mart employed more than one million people worldwide.

Wal-Mart has encountered some difficulty expanding its concept of discount mega-stores overseas. It began expanding

into foreign markets only in 1991, beginning with Mexico, where it experienced some difficulties in adapting to and understanding Mexican culture and consumer habits. Mexican consumers at the time preferred to buy Mexican goods rather than U.S. products, but Wal-Mart prioritized goods imported from the United States for a long time. Another early problem in Mexico was that people preferred to buy their food in small stores rather than in supermarkets. Wal-Mart had early losses in Argentina, Brazil, China, and Hong Kong for similar reasons.

Subsequently Wal-Mart has pursued a more successful foreign expansion strategy involving the purchase of existing chains. In Canada, Wal-Mart acquired a local chain, Woolco; Canada is Wal-Mart's most successful foreign operation. Wal-Mart has also purchased ASDA, a successful British retailer and grocery chain, to ease its entry into markets in Britain. "Our priorities are that we want to dominate North America first, then South America, and then Asia and then Europe," Wal-Mart's president and CEO David Glass told *USA Today* in 1998. According to Glass, everything that is done in Arkansas or Kansas can also be done in Brazil or China.

In 1984 Sam Walton, chairman of Wal-Mart, makes good on a promise to dance the hula when the company's pretax profits reached 8 percent.

Members of a group seeking better wages for Wal-Mart employees protest outside of a Wal-Mart in Nacogdoches, Texas, in November 2002.

In the United States Wal-Mart has expanded by offering ever-larger stores and expanded ranges of products. The largest stores are supercenters, carrying around 100,000 items. Supercenters combine grocery stores, general merchandise, and specialty shops like vision centers, Tire & Lube Expresses, restaurants, portrait studios, one-hour photo centers, hair salons, banks, and employment agencies under one massive roof. The first Wal-Mart supercenter opened in 1988 in Washington, Missouri, and the 1,000th opened in St. Robert, Missouri, in 2001.

The Richest Man in America

Separating the success of Wal-Mart from the personality of Sam Walton is impossible, Walton has been called the most driven businessman in America. Walton was famous for his Yogi Berra–style quips, his pearls of business wisdom, and for his extremely enthusiastic personality. His powerful personality helped Walton create a sense of camaraderie among his employees—he called them associates—which kept Wal-Mart's turnover rate much lower than the industry average. Walton personally visited every one of his stores, and Wal-Mart was one of the first retail chains to offer employee stock options.

Because most Wal-Mart stores were located in the Midwest, many living outside that region were unaware until 1984 of how large the Wal-Mart enterprise had become.

In that year *Forbes* magazine announced that Walton's 39 percent ownership of Wal-Mart stock made him the richest man in America. Subsequently, Walton was often questioned about why he did not display some of the more ostentatious trappings of his vast wealth. "We're not ashamed of having money, but I don't believe a big showy lifestyle is appropriate for everyone," he would reply. When a reporter questioned him about why he still drove a pickup truck, Walton responded, "Why do I drive a pickup truck? What am I supposed to haul my dogs around in, a Rolls-Royce?"

Money certainly did not change Walton's management style. When the company achieved pretax profits of 8 percent in 1984, Walton made good on a promise to company employees by doing the hula in a grass skirt at high noon on Wall Street. Walton also made each store responsible for donating a certain amount of money to local charities every year. The company currently donates well over $100 million every year to charity, making it the largest corporate donor in America.

Although Walton died in 1992, leaving his family a fortune estimated at $23.5 billion, the company is still run by Sam's folksy, down-to-earth, and business-savvy Ten Rules for Building a Business (see p. 1388). Wal-Mart dominates the discount retail industry by offering people products that they want, at competitive prices, in convenient locations for shopping. In 1999 Wal-Mart became the largest private employer in the world, with more than one million employees. On the day after Thanksgiving, 2002, the store enjoyed the single biggest sale day in history, taking in a record $1.5 billion.

Further Reading

Ortega, Bob. *In Sam We Trust: The Untold Story of Sam Walton and How Wal-Mart Is Devouring America.* New York: Times Business, 1998.

Vance, Sandra S., and Roy V. Scott. *Wal-Mart: A History of Sam Walton's Retail Phenomenon.* New York: Twayne Publishers, 1994.

Walton, Sam, with John Huey. *Sam Walton: Made in America.* New York: Doubleday, 1992.

—Lisa Magloff

Walt Disney Company

Generations of children have grown up with the creations of Walt Disney and his teams of animators and "imagineers." Along the way, the company has evolved from a small animation studio into an international multimedia and real estate conglomerate.

Born in Chicago in 1901, Walt Disney found refuge from his volatile father by immersing himself in art classes. He left home at age 16 to join the Red Cross Ambulance Corps during World War I. After the war he set up shop as a commercial artist and animator in Kansas City, Missouri. Business was not good, and in 1923, after he had been reduced to living in his studio and eating cold beans out of a can, Disney moved to Los Angeles to work with his older brother, Roy. The two brothers set up the Walt Disney Studios in the back of a real estate office in Hollywood.

Disney's first success was a cartoon series called *Oswald the Lucky Rabbit* (1927). Within a year, Disney made 26 Oswald cartoons, but he had unknowingly signed the rights over to his distributor; when Disney asked for more money, the distributor hired his own animators and began producing the series himself.

After the loss of Oswald, Disney and his chief animator Ub Iwerks created a new character—Mickey Mouse. The first two Mickey cartoons were silent, and Disney could not sell them. For the third cartoon, Disney and Iwerks used fully synchronized sound. *Steamboat Willie* opened to rave reviews in New York on November 18, 1928, and was an instant hit. In the days of static microphones, the sound and effects in the cartoon seemed much more lively than live action movies.

This early Mickey was very different from the round-faced, friendly Mickey we now know. The original Mickey had a leaner, harder look; he was brash and often cruel and mischievous. By the mid-1930s Disney had begun to soften the mouse's appearance and behavior. From then on, the company would also soften its corporate image to fit the artificial world it was creating. The often gruff Disney was transformed into kindly Uncle Walt. Studio publicity even implied that, just like Snow White's famous dwarfs, Walt Disney also whistled while he worked.

The company also learned the value of merchandising almost immediately. After *Steamboat Willie* was released, a New York businessman offered the company $300 for the license to put Mickey Mouse on some pencils he was manufacturing. Soon dolls, dishes, toothbrushes, radios, figurines, and a host of other products all bore Mickey's

See also:
Arts and Entertainment Industry; Miramax Films.

Walt Disney poses with his most famous creation in 1935.

likeness. The first Mickey Mouse book and newspaper comic strip were both published in 1930 to take advantage of the merchandizing boom.

The Mickey Mouse series was joined in 1929 by the Silly Symphonies. This series featured different casts of characters in each film and enabled the animators to experiment with stories that relied less on the gags and quick humor of the Mickey cartoons and more on mood, emotion, and musical themes. *Flowers and Trees*, a Silly Symphony and the first full-color cartoon, won the Academy Award for best cartoon for 1932, the first year that the Academy offered such a category. A Disney cartoon won the Oscar every year for the rest of the decade.

From Cartoons to Real Life

Disney embraced Technicolor as readily as he had embraced sound and, though Disney was a poor animator himself, he was a first-class gag man and story editor, and he constantly drove his growing team of enthusiastic artists to ever-greater sophistication of technique and expression. The company spent all its money making its first feature-length animation, *Snow White and the Seven Dwarfs*, released in 1937. The film was a spectacular hit and became the highest grossing film to that time. The intellectual and artistic communities hailed its populist authenticity as naive, courageous, and life affirming.

The studio lost most of its foreign market during World War II; such loss made turning a profit on expensive feature films like *Pinocchio* (1940), *Fantasia* (1940), and *Bambi* (1942) difficult. The studio slowed work and produced propaganda and training films for the military. When the war ended, the Disney Studio regained its prewar footing by releasing packages of features—films made up of short cartoons packaged together, as well as live action features like *Song of the South* (1946) and *Treasure Island* (1950).

Not content with creating an artificial world on the screen, Disney established a studio of imagineers to bring the unthreatening world of cartoons to life in three dimensions. The company again invested almost everything it had to build Disneyland, the world's first theme park. The park opened in 1955 and was an instant success.

Walt Disney died on December 15, 1966, but Roy Disney continued to run Disney Studios according to Walt's principles. *The Love Bug*, released in 1969, was the highest grossing film of that year. Walt Disney World, another of Walt's projects, opened near Orlando on October 1, 1971. After Roy Disney's death in late 1971, a team including Card Walker, Donn Tatum, and Ron Miller—all originally trained by the Disney brothers—ran the company.

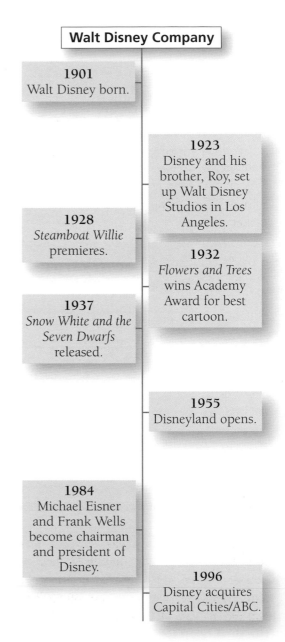

Walt Disney Company

1901
Walt Disney born.

1923
Disney and his brother, Roy, set up Walt Disney Studios in Los Angeles.

1928
Steamboat Willie premieres.

1932
Flowers and Trees wins Academy Award for best cartoon.

1937
Snow White and the Seven Dwarfs released.

1955
Disneyland opens.

1984
Michael Eisner and Frank Wells become chairman and president of Disney.

1996
Disney acquires Capital Cities/ABC.

During the 1970s and early 1980s audiences were diminishing for the family films that had been the mainstay of the company for many years, and Disney was not attracting the huge teenage and adult market. The theme parks continued to prosper, however, with the opening of EPCOT (Experimental Prototype Community of Tomorrow) in 1979 and Tokyo Disneyland in 1982.

Disney Studios was experiencing diminishing box-office returns; however, it retained many assets, including the studios and theme parks. The growing perception in the financial community that Disney stock was undervalued in relation to the company's assets led, in 1983, to an attempted takeover of the company by corporate raiders.

Tomorrowland

The efforts to keep the company from being broken up and sold ended in 1984 when Michael Eisner and Frank Wells became chairman and president, respectively. Eisner had been president and chief operating officer of Paramount Pictures Corporation and had never even seen a Disney movie until he was an adult. He and Wells began bringing Disney back into the mainstream. They raised ticket prices at the theme parks, put out scores of vintage Disney animated films on videocassette, and built Disney's live-action studio from a Hollywood afterthought into a box-office leader by creating Walt Disney Studio Entertainment, the film production and distribution division of the Walt Disney Company, and opening two new film divisions, Touchstone Pictures and Hollywood Pictures. Without the Disney name, these divisions were able to produce different styles of material and even make R-rated films.

The live-action and animated titles are produced through Walt Disney Pictures, Touchstone, and Hollywood Pictures as well as independent film-oriented Miramax. Disney's Buena Vista distribution unit is the world's top movie distributor. Disney also gained more control over its marketing and merchandising by purchasing Childcraft, a chain of children's stores, and by opening the highly successful and profitable chain of

The Magic Castle at Walt Disney World in Orlando, Florida.

Disney Stores. By 1996 the company owned more than 450 Disney Stores.

Disney has also moved into publishing, forming Hyperion Books, Hyperion Books for Children, and Disney Press, which released books on Disney and non-Disney subjects. In 1991 Disney purchased *Discover* magazine, the leading consumer science monthly. In 1993 Disney was awarded the franchise for a National Hockey League team, the Mighty Ducks of Anaheim, and soon after released *The Mighty Ducks* movie. The company also purchased a stake in the California Angels baseball team.

Although Disneyland Paris (opened on April 12, 1992) initially lost a great deal of money, Disney has continued to add new theme parks, hotels, resorts, campgrounds, and even an entire town—Celebration,

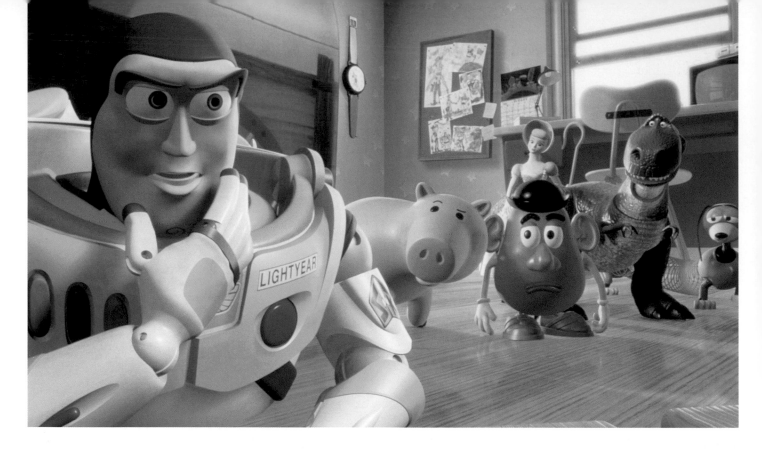

A scene from Toy Story *(1995), a film made by Pixar in partnership with Disney.*

Florida. Billed as an antidote to suburban sprawl and a return to traditional small-town America, Celebration was a 5,000-acre experiment in town planning, emphasizing higher-density building and downtown centers as key ingredients. The town resembles a scene out of a cheerful 1950s movie, and its gaily painted clapboard houses were snapped up quickly.

The death of Wells in a helicopter accident in 1994 led to the eventual firing of movie studio head Jeffrey Katzenberg, who had made an ill-timed bid for Wells's job. Instead of Katzenberg, Eisner chose former Creative Artists Agency head Michael Ovitz as the new president of Disney. Katzenberg went on to cofound Dreamworks Studio, but his $350 million lawsuit against Eisner and Disney pitted the biggest names in Hollywood against each other. Eisner's later firing of Ovitz was one of the messiest in Hollywood memory. The two firings likely cost the company more than $350 million in settlements.

Following these lawsuits, many Hollywood watchers considered Disney to be in decline. The roar of the mouse was heard again in early 1996, when Disney completed its acquisition of Capital Cities/ABC, the top television network in the United States. The $19 billion transaction was the second largest in U.S. history and brought Disney 10 TV stations, 21 radio stations, seven daily newspapers, and ownership positions in four cable networks. The success of *Toy Story 2* and ABC's *Who Wants to Be a Millionaire?* put Disney back on top: in 2000, Disney's $22 billion in annual sales made it the world's largest media company at the time.

Further Reading

Connellan, Tom. *Inside the Magic Kingdom*. Austin, Tex.: Bard Press, 1997.

Flower, Joe. *Prince of the Magic Kingdom: Michael Eisner and the Re-making of Disney*. New York: John Wiley and Sons, 1991.

Frantz, Doug, and Catherine Collins. *Celebration, U.S.A.* New York: Henry Holt, 2000.

Grover, Ron. *The Disney Touch: Disney, ABC, & the Quest for the World's Greatest Media Empire*. Chicago: Irwin, 1997.

Thomas, Bob. *Building a Company: Roy O. Disney and the Creation of an Entertainment Empire*. New York: Hyperion, 1998.

Watts, Steven. *The Magic Kingdom: Walt Disney and the American Way of Life*. Boston: Houghton Mifflin, 1997.

—*Lisa Magloff*

Wealth Distribution

The issue of wealth distribution has dominated world history for hundreds of years. It has been the cause of wars, revolutions, and dramatic political changes across the globe. These conflicts resulted in new forms of government and affected the lives of billions of people. The distribution of wealth is how the income, property, and productive resources of a society are apportioned among its members. A society with an equal distribution of wealth would see all citizens with the same amount.

Historical Perspective

Most of history has featured a dramatically unequal distribution of wealth worldwide, with a small number controlling the vast majority of the wealth. In kingdoms with larger populations, for example, China, Japan, and most of Europe, such control was maintained through a system called feudalism. In brief, feudalism involved the rulers granting land to nobles in exchange for loyalty; the nobles then allowed peasants residency in return for working the land, paying taxes, and serving as soldiers.

The poor benefited because they received protection provided by the nobles. The cost of this system to the poor was twofold. First was a rigid social structure in which the peasants had no political rights. Second, as few employment opportunities were available outside of farming and peasants were not free to leave the estates, feudalism kept the great majority of the peasants poor. The feudal system worked to the great advantage of the land-owning nobles.

Feudalism gradually evolved into less onerous forms of government, with peasants slowly gaining some rights in Europe as the Crusades, the growth of cities, and other events unfolded. This trend accelerated with the beginning of the Agricultural Revolution, starting about 1500. Farm production increased because of better technology, new crops, and better farming methods. By the 1700s increased agricultural efficiencies led to a surplus labor force because fewer farmers were needed. About the same time, the Industrial Revolution began and the poor migrated to the cities to work in the new factories.

Conditions in the cities were abysmal: low pay, unsafe working conditions, and long hours. Rapid urbanization, first in England and then in other parts of Europe, was accompanied by the creation of slums and unsanitary living conditions. However,

See also:
Globalization; Income Distribution.

An 1873 wood engraving entitled "Two Christmas Dinners," from Frank Leslie's Illustrated Newspaper, *shows the contrast between rich and poor in the nineteenth century.*

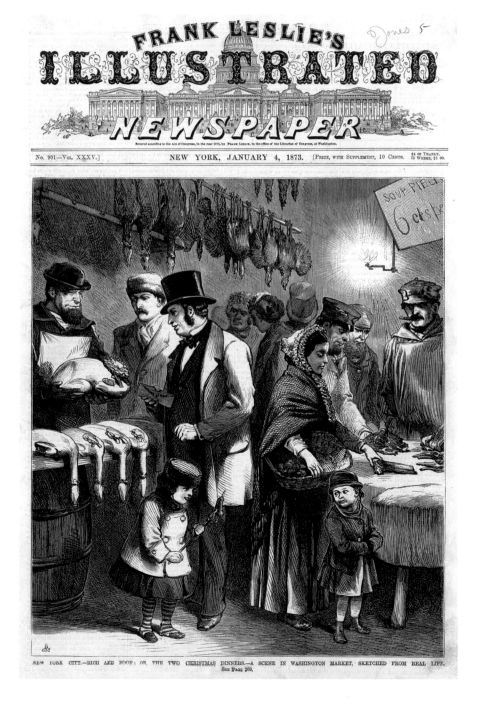

NEW YORK CITY.—HIGH AND POOR; OR, THE TWO CHRISTMAS DINNERS.—A SCENE IN WASHINGTON MARKET, SKETCHED FROM REAL LIFE.
See Page 269.

another consequence of the Industrial Revolution was the rise of a new social class, the newly rich. These were men who became wealthy by starting their own businesses. Such means of generating wealth had dramatic political and economic effects on Europe and the United States.

Many of the newly rich embraced a political philosophy called liberalism. Most prominently asserted by Adam Smith (1723–1790), liberalism called for less government interference in the economy and increased economic freedoms. The liberals also demanded political rights from the ruling conservatives, which resulted in the gradual spread of male suffrage, the right to vote. The gradual redistribution of wealth during the Industrial Revolution led to greater political rights for the newly rich and greater economic opportunities for all. However, liberals shared many of the attitudes the "old money" held about the poor: both felt that poverty was a natural condition and that the solution to being poor was hard work. Thus, neither liberals nor conservatives offered a direct solution to the mass poverty of the urban slums.

A second and related consequence was the development of Marxism. Karl Marx (1818–1883) was repulsed by liberalism and considered it to be a way to continue the suffering of the proletariat—his term for the large majority who were the working poor. He forecast that this system would eventually fall to a worldwide revolt of the poor in response to their horrid conditions of life and labor. Marxism called for a drastic change in the distribution of political power and wealth in society. In brief, Marx argued for total economic and political equality, with universal suffrage and public ownership of all means of production. Such changes were to be accomplished through a violent overthrow of the rich by the poor.

Marx's predictions of worldwide revolution were not realized for several reasons. First, Adam Smith's assertion that liberalism would ultimately improve living standards for the poor and middle class proved to be correct. Gradually the working hours, pay, and working conditions of European and U.S. workers improved. Second, the capitalist nations gradually enacted social and economic reforms to address the worst excesses of capitalism. Voting rights were expanded in Europe and the United States, child labor laws enacted, and other laws passed to improve working conditions and living standards for the poor.

Wealth Distribution in the Modern Era

Economists generally agree that, at least in developed countries, wealth gradually became more equally distributed until roughly 1970. Government policies like unemployment insurance, old age insurance (pensions), and progressive income tax codes all worked to redistribute wealth, benefiting the poor more than the rich. This period also saw the "golden age" of the middle class, especially in the United States. The country experienced an extended economic expansion after World War II, maintaining high levels of employment.

U.S. Aggregate Income: Percentage Received by Each Fifth of Households 1970 to 2000						
Year	Lowest fifth	Second fifth	Third fifth	Fourth fifth	Highest fifth	Top 5 percent
1970	4.1	10.8	17.4	24.5	43.3	16.6
1975	4.4	10.5	17.1	24.8	43.2	15.9
1980	4.3	10.3	16.9	24.9	43.7	15.8
1985	4.0	9.7	16.3	24.6	45.3	17.0
1990	3.9	9.6	15.9	24.0	46.6	18.6
1995	3.7	9.1	15.2	23.3	48.7	21.0
2000	3.6	8.9	14.9	23.0	49.6	21.9

Source: U.S. Bureau of the Census, Current Population Survey, http://www.census.gov/hhes/www/income.html (April 29, 2003).

Combined with relatively strong unions, workers maintained high wages that ensured good living standards.

The early 1970s brought economic instability and other changes in the economy. Inflation eroded the purchasing power of consumers, hurting the poor the most. Concurrently, foreign competition eroded the profits of U.S. and European corporations, reducing their ability to pay high wages. Previously well-paid manufacturing jobs were moved to developing nations as corporations attempted to cut costs.

About the same time the nature of work began to change. Service sector jobs, for example, in health care and tourism, grew as manufacturing declined. Employers began to demand more sophisticated skills, especially computer usage, in return for high wages. The result of these changes was reduced opportunity for low-skilled workers to earn middle-class wages. Unions, which previously had been able to force employers to pay higher wages, were weaker in these fields. Unions also experienced a general decline in their overall power because of political changes and the decline of manufacturing jobs.

Determining Wealth

Education has become the most important predictor of a worker's income and potential to become wealthy. The average earnings chart above shows that in every case, more education results in a higher average income for all workers. For example, the income difference between the average college graduate and high school graduate is roughly $27,000 for men and $14,000 for women.

The chart above also highlights two other points. First, those who earn the most on average have advanced degrees in law, medicine, and other fields. Second, it also shows a dramatic difference between the earnings of men and women. Many factors account for this, including women having a more prominent role in child rearing, as well as a pay bias toward men in some fields.

The chart may also lead to the conclusion that income and wealth are concentrated

Average Earnings by Educational Attainment 1999					
	No high school diploma	High school diploma only	Bachelor's degree	Master's degree	Doctorate
Male	$18,855	$30,414	$57,706	$68,367	$97,357
Female	$12,145	$18,092	$32,546	$42,378	$61,136

Note: Year-round, full-time workers.
Source: U.S. Bureau of the Census, *Current Population Survey,* http://www.census.gov/hhes/www/income.html (April 29, 2003).

in the hands of the most educated. However, this is not entirely the case. Studies indicate that although some of the richest individuals in the United States are highly educated doctors, lawyers, and so on, most are not members of the intellectual elite, nor are they children who inherited large estates. The majority of the wealthiest Americans are first-generation rich—those who have started and run their own businesses.

The explosion of wealth in Silicon Valley, California, the center of computer industry innovation, illustrates this trend. The second half of the 1990s witnessed a tremendous business boom in Internet applications and a concurrent expansion in start-up companies creating new software. Most of these companies were founded

Economic Mobility in the United States

A fundamental premise of the U.S. economy is that all citizens have the opportunity to improve their economic well-being. This important idea suggests a relationship between work and income that gives people an incentive to work hard to get ahead.

Economic mobility measures how often Americans increase or decrease their incomes compared with national averages. Economic mobility is measured in quintiles, or fifths, of the U.S. working population. Thus, the top quintile is the richest 20 percent of Americans.

Personal income changes over the average person's lifetime. In general, income rises with age, education, and work experience, and peaks in a person's forties and fifties. After this point people generally move down in income quintiles because of retirement or reduction in working hours.

Studies of the American economy indicate substantial economic mobility. Between 25 and 33 percent of adults move into a new income quintile each year; over the course of a decade, 60 percent move into a new tax bracket. Thus, the poor can increase their incomes and the rich can fall back. The total rate of mobility has remained constant for the past several decades: the fortunes of specific individuals change often, the proportion of people in each quintile has remained stable. Overall opportunity has not increased despite numerous government initiatives.

Factors Leading to Increased Inequitable Wealth Distribution in the United States after 1970

- Inflation eroded purchasing power, affecting poor most.
- Foreign competition eroded U.S. businesses' ability to pay high wages.
- Well-paid manufacturing jobs moved to developing nations.
- General decline in power of unions prevented them from forcing higher pay.
- Shift to Information Age economy reduced opportunity of low-skilled workers to earn middle-class wages.

by people with middle-class backgrounds who had four years of college or less. This group was unique more for its talent and energy than formal education—many of them had dropped out of college, or did not attend at all.

Technology companies competed for the best employees by using stock options (the right for employees to buy ownership). The combination of luck, talent, and hard work, as well as a concurrent stock market boom, resulted in many of these entrepreneurs becoming extremely wealthy before they turned 30.

The rapid pace of change in the computer industry illustrates an important point about wealth in the United States. Wealth can be obtained through hard work and talent, but once a family becomes wealthy it will not necessarily remain so. In most cases, family fortunes do not last beyond the second or third generation. Many of the dot-com millionaires lost their fortunes with the dot-crash of 2000.

The stock market collapse raises the issue of stock ownership as a means of wealth generation. Roughly 50 percent of Americans have invested in the stock market as a means to build wealth. The rich tend to have far more invested, and thus see greater changes in their fortune with the movements of the markets. Such volatility is partly responsible for the widening gap between rich and poor in the 1990s and a shrinking of this gap with the stock market declines that followed. Despite the vicissitudes of the market, over the long term the trend of greater stock ownership should allow for more Americans to build wealth.

Global Distribution of Wealth

The distribution of wealth can also be considered both internally—distribution within one nation—and between countries. The global distribution of wealth is starkly unequal. For the purposes of study, nations are usually divided into three kinds. The first are called developed nations, which include the countries of western Europe, the United States, Canada, Japan, South Korea, and Taiwan. In general, these nations are comparatively wealthy because they industrialized successfully. As a result, their living standards and incomes tend to be the highest in the world.

The second tier of nations includes some that are in the process of industrializing or that have wealth from exporting oil. This group includes Mexico, Saudi Arabia, and much of eastern Europe. The remaining countries are referred to as lesser- (or under-) developed nations. In general, the average income is well below $1,000 per year and

Aggregate Income of Selected Nations: Percentage Share by Each Fifth of Households 1998

	Lowest fifth	Second fifth	Third fifth	Fourth fifth	Highest fifth
Austria	10.4	14.8	18.5	22.9	33.3
Brazil	2.5	5.7	9.9	17.7	64.2
China	5.5	9.8	14.9	22.3	47.5
India	9.2	13.0	16.8	21.7	39.3
Italy	7.6	12.9	17.3	23.2	38.9
Mexico	4.1	7.8	12.5	20.2	55.3
Nigeria	4.0	8.9	14.4	23.4	49.4
United States	4.8	10.5	16.0	23.5	45.2

Source: The World Bank, World Development Report, 1998–1999.

Percent of Population Living on Less than $1 per Day 1990 to 1998

Region	1990	1993	1996	1998
East Asia and the Pacific	66.1	60.5	48.6	49.1
Eastern Europe and Central Asia	57.3	51.6	42.8	45.0
Latin America and the Caribbean	38.1	35.1	37.0	36.4
Middle East and North Africa	24.8	24.1	22.2	21.9
South Asia	86.8	85.4	85.0	84.0
Sub-Saharan Africa	76.4	77.8	76.9	75.6
World	**61.7**	**60.1**	**56.1**	**56.0**

Source: Chandrika Kaul, *Statistical Handbook on the World's Children*, Westport, Conn., Oryx Press, 2002.

quality of life measures are far behind those of the more advanced countries.

The table on page 1398 gives aggregate income data from eight countries, showing the share of income received by each quintile of society; the first fifth represents the poorest and the highest the richest. This table reveals several facts. Most dramatically, no nation in the world has an equal distribution of income. Austria comes the closest, and even in that country the richest 20 percent earn more than three times the income of the poorest 20 percent. The higher the income bracket a person occupies, the greater amount of income received.

The second trend shown by this table is that the poorer the country, the more concentrated the income is in the top fifth. For example, the richest 20 percent of Brazil's population earns roughly twice as much as the other 80 percent of Brazilians. The wealthy have several economic advantages in poorer countries. One is access to education—many poor countries are unable to offer free public education to all citizens. Another is that poor countries tend to have corrupt governments dominated by the rich. Thus the wealthy get richer and the poor are kept from gaining ground.

Wealthier nations generally operate on principles that reduce wealth inequalities in society. All have democratic governments and varying depth of commitment to the idea of addressing wealth inequities through government spending and taxation policies. These traditions are strongest in Europe and

Japan and are somewhat weaker in the United States.

Experts disagree about the future of the world's wealth distribution. Some are pessimistic, asserting that the decline of well-paying manufacturing jobs and other changes in the nature of work suggest that only the highly educated will prosper in the future. Others are optimistic, arguing that governments now have a much better understanding of poverty and are undertaking programs to mitigate it. Moreover, they maintain that advances in medicine and other areas do improve the quality of life for the poor, as will the spread of democracy and capitalism. In either case, neither group predicts a solution to poverty or a dramatic change in how the wealth of the world's countries is apportioned. The highly educated and entrepreneurial will continue to do well, while the less educated and unfortunate will lag behind.

Further Reading

Galbraith, John Kenneth. *The Affluent Society*. Boston: Houghton Mifflin, 1998.

Heilbroner, Robert. *The Worldly Philosophers: The Lives, Times and Ideas of the Great Economic Thinkers*. 7th ed. New York: Simon & Schuster, 1999.

Reich, Robert. *The Work of Nations: Preparing Ourselves for 21st Century Capitalism*. New York: Vintage Books, 1991.

Stanley, Thomas J., and William D. Danko. *The Millionaire Next Door: The Surprising Secrets of America's Wealthy*. New York: MJF Books, 2002.

—*David Long*

See also:

Capitalism; Division of Labor; Mercantilism; Smith, Adam.

Wealth of Nations, The

An Inquiry into the Nature and Causes of the Wealth of Nations (1776) was written by the Scots moral philosopher and political economist Adam Smith (1723–1790). Widely acknowledged as the foundation text of modern economics, *The Wealth of Nations* is also one of the key works of eighteenth-century Enlightenment liberalism.

Smith's aim in writing *The Wealth of Nations* was to explain why some economies were demonstrably more successful than others at generating economic growth. Why, for example, did the living standards of some European peasants exceed those of African kings? Smith's explanation rests on two essentially anthropological assumptions: first, that humans are unique in their natural predisposition to create a complex web of economic interdependence by trading with one another; and, second, that individuals, while capable of altruism toward others, are motivated principally by self-interest. A society's capacity for wealth creation therefore depends on the extent to which its economic organization works with, rather than against, these core human characteristics.

Smith concludes that a society derives important advantages from the adoption of two specific principles of economic organization. The first of these principles is the division of labor into increasingly specialized tasks. Using the now-famous example of a pin factory, Smith lists three ways in which specialization boosts labor productivity: workers develop greater skill at their assigned task; no time is wasted moving from one task to another; and specialized workers are more likely to devise mechanical innovations because "some one or other of those who are employed in each particular branch of labour should soon find out easier and readier methods of performing their own particular work, wherever the nature of it admits of such improvement." In Smith's analysis, the division of labor is the foundation of economic interdependence: "The woolen coat, for example, which covers the day-labourer, as coarse and rough as it may appear, is the produce of the joint labour of a great multitude of workmen."

The second principle of economic organization commended by Smith is the free market, or laissez-faire—an idea he adapted from a French school of economic thought known as physiocracy. Smith conceives of the free market as an "invisible hand" that guides the individual's self-interest toward the public benefit. In a free market, producers compete against one another to supply goods to consumers at the prices they are prepared to pay, thereby empowering the consumer and promoting economic efficiency. Furthermore, the opportunities for labor specialization increase as the scope of the market broadens, resulting in additional productivity gains.

Smith's faith in the efficacy of markets was not absolute. He argues for governmental provision in three specific areas: the provision of national defense, the administration of justice, and the supply of socially necessary goods and services "of such a nature, that the profit [to those who might produce them] could never repay the expense to any individual or small number of individuals"—what modern economists call "public goods," for example, urban sanitation.

Smith also concedes that "people of the same trade seldom meet together, even for merriment and diversion, but the conversation ends in a conspiracy against the public, or in some contrivance to raise prices." This

---

Key Ideas of *The Wealth of Nations*

- Free exercise of economic self-interest creates the greatest prosperity for a nation.
- Regulations limiting economic freedom should be abolished.
- Division of labor boosts labor productivity and is the foundation of economic interdependence.
- The free market is the "invisible hand" that guides individual self-interest toward the public good.

The Wealth of Nations
(Excerpt)

Every individual is continually exerting himself to find out the most advantageous employment for whatever capital he can command. It is his own advantage, indeed, and not that of the society, which he has in view. But the study of his own advantage naturally, or rather necessarily, leads him to prefer that employment which is most advantageous to the society. . . .

[T]he annual revenue of every society is always precisely equal to the exchangeable value of the whole annual produce of its industry, or rather is precisely the same thing with that exchangeable value. As every individual, therefore, endeavours as much as he can both to employ his capital in the support of domestic industry, and so to direct that industry that its produce may be of the greatest value; every individual necessarily labours to render the annual revenue of the society as great as he can. He generally, indeed, neither intends to promote the public interest, nor knows how much he is promoting it. By preferring the support of domestic to that of foreign industry, he intends only his own security; and by directing that industry in such a manner as its produce may be of the greatest value, he intends only his own gain, and he is in this, as in many other cases, led by an invisible hand to promote an end which was no part of his intention. Nor is it always the worse for the society that it was no part of it. By pursuing his own interest he frequently promotes that of the society more effectually than when he really intends to promote it. . . .

What is prudence in the conduct of every private family can scarce be folly in that of a great kingdom. If a foreign country can supply us with a commodity cheaper than we ourselves can make it, better buy it of them with some part of the produce of our own industry employed in a way in which we have some advantage. The general industry of the country, being always in proportion to the capital which employs it, will not thereby be diminished, no more than that of the above-mentioned artificers; but only left to find out the way in which it can be employed with the greatest advantage. It is certainly not employed to the greatest advantage when it is thus directed towards an object which it can buy cheaper than it can make. The value of its annual produce is certainly more or less diminished when it is thus turned away from producing commodities evidently of more value than the commodity which it is directed to produce. According to the supposition, that commodity could be purchased from foreign countries cheaper than it can be made at home. It could, therefore, have been purchased with a part only of the commodities, or, what is the same thing, with a part only of the price of the commodities, which the industry employed by an equal capital would have produced at home, had it been left to follow its natural course. The industry of the country, therefore, is thus turned away from a more to a less advantageous employment, and the exchangeable value of its annual produce, instead of being increased, according to the intention of the lawgiver, must necessarily be diminished by every such regulation.

Source: Adam Smith, *An Inquiry into the Nature and Causes of the Wealth of Nations,* http://www.econlib.org/library/Smith/smWN1.html (March 21, 2003).

passage has often been cited in defense of government antitrust legislation. However, Smith himself wrote that the law could not realistically prevent collusion between producers, though "it ought to do nothing to facilitate such assemblies, much less to render them necessary."

At the time of its publication (coinciding with the printing of the Declaration of Independence), *The Wealth of Nations* was a revolutionary text, aiming at nothing less than the intellectual demolition of the prevailing economic theory and practice of mercantilism, according to which economic growth was the responsibility of the state. Smith's ideas, elaborated upon and modified by later economists working in the liberal tradition, now constitute the economic assumptions on which the advanced industrial world operates. These ideas are also now establishing themselves in post-communist countries and in the developing world. *The Wealth of Nations* is one of the most enduringly influential texts in the history of the social sciences.

Further Reading

Heilbroner, Robert. *The Worldly Philosophers.* 7th ed. New York: Simon & Schuster, 1999.

Smith, Adam. *The Wealth of Nations.* 1776. Reprint, New York: Everyman's Library, 1991.

—*Peter C. Grosvenor*

See also:
Corporate Social
Responsibility; General
Electric.

Welch, Jack

1935–
Chairman of General Electric, 1981–2001

Jack Welch, retired chairman and chief executive officer of General Electric (GE), earned worldwide respect when he transformed a stodgy and aging company into one of the best-managed and most-profitable organizations in U.S. industry. Because of his quick and decisive responses to the challenges of emerging global markets, he is regarded as the forerunner of industrial reconstruction.

Born John F. Welch on November 19, 1935, in Peabody, Massachusetts, Welch was raised in the town of Salem. He credits his strength of character and purposefulness in life to the strong influence of his mother, Grace. A tough-talking daughter of immigrants, Grace never finished high school but took great pride in rearing Jack, her only child. She encouraged him in school and instilled a fierce competitiveness. Grace liked to stress the importance of being in charge of one's own destiny. Above all, she taught her son to speak honestly and see things as they really are, lessons Welch says he has carried with him all his life.

Just as important were the lessons of Welch's father. The senior Welch, also a child of immigrants and a man with a grade school education, worked as a railroad conductor. He had a strong work ethic, never missing a day at the railroad. If the weather looked threatening, he would have his wife drive him to the station the night before and he would sleep in a railroad car to ensure that he would be on the job in the morning.

As a child, Welch played baseball, basketball, and football. In high school he was a starter on the hockey team and a regular caddy at the country club. On the greens, he rubbed shoulders with the well-to-do, which taught Welch about human behavior; he noticed that some people say and do the right things while others do not, regardless of their socioeconomic class. Many observers attribute much of Welch's success to his good instincts about people, knowing who to cultivate and who to ignore.

Welch's parents and teachers were eager for him to attend college. Welch attended the University of Massachusetts, a choice he believes was preferable to the Ivy League where he says the strong academic competition would not have allowed him to become a star student. Welch majored in chemical engineering, graduated at the top of his class, and went on to earn a master's and a doctorate from the University of Illinois.

After graduation, Welch and his new wife, Carolyn, a graduate student, contemplated their future. Welch knew that he liked people better than books and sports better than science, so he determined not to spend his life in a lab. When GE offered him a position in Massachusetts in 1960, he and Carolyn headed back to his home state and life in corporate America.

Welch thrived in the world of industry. He developed close, enduring friendships

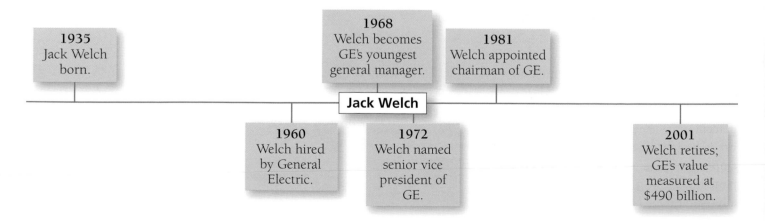

1935
Jack Welch born.

1960
Welch hired by General Electric.

Jack Welch

1968
Welch becomes GE's youngest general manager.

1972
Welch named senior vice president of GE.

1981
Welch appointed chairman of GE.

2001
Welch retires; GE's value measured at $490 billion.

with his superiors and moved steadily up the corporate ladder. In 1968, at the age of 33, he was GE's youngest general manager. He was named senior vice president in 1972, and nine years later, he was tapped to lead GE. As a longtime insider, Welch understood well the weaknesses of the company's corporate structure, its layers of bureaucracy, and its lack of flexibility. He grabbed the wheel as chief executive officer and switched the company into high gear, ripping and tearing at established people and practices.

Welch removed layers of middle management, and he insisted that every year, the least-effective employees, the bottom 10 percent, in every part of the organization be fired. Welch rewarded good managers by empowering them to make decisions independently and meeting with them annually—he met with more than 15,000 GE

managers during his tenure—for long, feisty, in-your-face exchanges of ideas. At the same time he was reducing his workforce, he expanded operations with more than 600 acquisitions.

His critics were baffled: Why fix a company that isn't broken? Welch foresaw what

Jack Welch, left, speaks with reporters in 1997.

Globalization is the best chance in the world for the have-nots to become haves. Look at Ireland 20 years ago—it had nothing. American businesses came there. Today Ireland is thriving, with great GDP growth, great income per capita.

Globalization has not solved all the world's problems. It has not cured cancer. It has clearly not reached parts of the subcontinent. It didn't reach Afghanistan. I understand some critics' views of globalization: labor unions in developed countries; the threat of losing jobs. I don't understand the environmentalists' view of it, because every place you go you bring world-class standards, and you put factories in that are better than anything in the country. The neighborhood gets better.

Globalization has done better than the U.N. and a zillion other organizations in improving lives. Go to Prague, Budapest and East Berlin. People are living far better than they ever dreamt, and it's because of globalization.

—Jack Welch, addressing the Commonwealth Club of California, November 2001

A businessman browses through the Japanese edition of Welch's autobiography, Jack: Straight from the Gut, *at a Tokyo bookstore in 2002. The book made the* New York Times *best-seller list and became a hot seller in Japan.*

many did not, and he addressed potential problems immediately and somewhat ruthlessly, earning a reputation as the toughest boss in America. His overhaul of GE was not without controversy. In the 1980s Welch eliminated more than 100,000 jobs, earning the nickname "Neutron Jack," after the neutron bomb, which leaves buildings standing but wipes out humans. Welch also became notorious for sending work overseas, reportedly commenting that "in an ideal world, every plant you own would be on a barge." The success of Welch's strategy is indisputable. One year after he took the reins, GE's profits had risen by 9 percent, to $1.7 billion. By the time Welch retired in 2001, the value of GE had risen from about $14 billion to roughly $490 billion.

Welch's image as the ideal CEO was tarnished somewhat in 2002, when the terms of his extravagant retirement package were revealed: an annual pension of $9 million, an apartment in New York City renting for $80,000 a month, and satellite television services for Welch's five homes. Under fire from the media and from GE shareholders, Welch renounced the most opulent elements of the package, promising to pay for them himself in the future.

Welch earned many honors in his 20 years as CEO at GE. Three times he was voted by his peers as most respected CEO in an *Industry Week* poll. *Business Week* said he was the gold standard by which other CEOs are measured. The Welch legacy is bolstered by the popularity of many books outlining his management philosophy. With titles like *Get Better or Get Beaten!* (1994) and *Control Your Destiny or Someone Else Will* (1993), these best-sellers describe Welch and his ideals.

Further Reading

Slater, Robert. *Get Better or Get Beaten!: 29 Leadership Secrets from GE's Jack Welch.* 2nd ed. New York: McGraw-Hill, 2001.

———. *Jack Welch and the G.E. Way: Management Insights and Leadership Secrets of the Legendary CEO.* New York: McGraw-Hill, 1999.

Tichy, Noel M., and Stratford Sherman. *Control Your Destiny or Someone Else Will: How Jack Welch Is Making General Electric the World's Most Competitive Corporation.* New York: HarperBusiness, 1994.

Welch, Jack, and John A. Byrne. *Jack: Straight from the Gut.* New York: Warner Books, 2001.

—*Karen Ehrle*

Wells Fargo

In 2002 Wells Fargo was the fifth largest bank in the United States, the product of more than 2,000 mergers over 150 years of business. The company's trademark Concord stagecoaches, pulled by six horses, have become one of the most recognizable brands in banking, while also evoking Wells Fargo's pivotal role in the history of the American West.

Wells Fargo began as the western counterpart to another well-known company, American Express. In 1850 Livingston, Fargo & Company, founded in 1845 by Henry Wells and William G. Fargo, merged with two other companies to create American Express, an express business based on the East Coast that made money by undercutting the U.S. Postal Service. Henry Wells sought to expand American Express westward and establish a banking and transportation outpost in San Francisco to capitalize on California's Gold Rush. When the board of American Express vetoed the expansion, Wells and Fargo started their own company while retaining their positions with American Express. On July 13, 1852, the newly formed Wells, Fargo & Company opened its first West Coast office, in San Francisco, soon expanding to Sacramento and Stockton.

Wells Fargo's early services included buying and transporting gold, cashing checks, selling exchanges, accepting deposits, and making loans. The bank would send men on horseback to the gold camps to buy gold dust to be delivered to the East, and the Wells Fargo coaches would travel the 2,700-mile Southern Overland Route, stretching from San Francisco to St. Louis, Missouri, via Los Angeles and El Paso, Texas. The route was moved north, through Salt Lake City, Utah, and Denver, Colorado, during the Civil War. By the mid-1850s Wells Fargo had become the largest express company in the nation, with 1,500 horses and 150 Concord coaches, which are now often referred to as the Rolls Royce of stagecoaches.

Within three years Wells Fargo was the second-largest commercial bank in San Francisco, and it soon grew to nearly 10,000 branches nationwide. Wells Fargo began its ocean-to-ocean service in 1888, becoming the first express service to ship all varieties of valuables transcontinentally. In 1905 the company made the first of many mergers, with Nevada National Bank, and moved its headquarters to New York City.

Wells Fargo continued to grow until World War I, when, as a wartime measure, the U.S. government took control of the nation's railroad and express services, merging Wells Fargo, American Express, and the other national services into the American Railway Express. This left Wells Fargo with just one banking outpost in San Francisco, with 80 employees and $37 million in assets. In its new banking-only form, Wells Fargo pursued commercial markets, while American Express re-formed its business for financial services for travelers.

In 1923 Wells Fargo merged with the Union Trust Company. The new bank was able to pay dividends throughout the Great Depression, an accomplishment that

See also:
American Express Company;
Santa Fe Trail.

A Wells Fargo Express office in Virginia City, Nevada, in 1866.

The Wells Fargo Deadwood Treasure Wagon, transporting $250,000 of gold bullion under armed guard from the Great Homestake Mine, Deadwood, South Dakota, in 1890.

acquired Barclays Bank of California. By 1989 the Hong Kong and Shanghai Banking Corporation was handling overseas banking for Wells Fargo customers.

Wells Fargo was making advances on other fronts. Through collaboration with Prodigy in 1989, Wells Fargo became a pioneer in online banking. Online banking and other Wells Fargo innovations, including 24-hour telephone banking, widespread ATMs, and point-of-sale banking, have become standard, but at the time they were cutting edge. Wells Fargo had put in place the technology—the Wells Electronic Banking System (WEBS), an early model of real-time computer bookkeeping—that

few other financial institutions could match. Nevertheless, the Wells Fargo name slipped into the background for nearly 30 years, becoming just one of many banks in the United States.

After a merger with the American Trust Company in the early 1960s, Wells Fargo began opening branch offices and started turning to retail banking, growing from a dozen offices to more than 100, mostly in northern California. During the 1970s chairman and chief executive officer (CEO) Richard Cooley pushed Wells Fargo into international markets. When Cooley resigned in 1982, Carl Reichardt, then president of Wells Fargo, took over as CEO, pulling Wells Fargo back into retail banking and, in turn, back into the public eye.

Reichardt believed that banks should be run like fast-food restaurants—with consistent service, low prices, and a limited menu—and he became known for his cold, but successful, efficiency. During Reichardt's tenure, Wells Fargo reduced its staff and acquired assets aggressively. In 1986 Wells Fargo merged with Crocker National Bank, giving Wells Fargo the presence in southern California that it had lacked. More than 1,600 Crocker employees were laid off in the process, but the $1.08 billion merger made Wells Fargo the tenth largest bank in the United States, with assets of more than $40 billion. The following year Wells Fargo acquired the personal trust business of Bank of America; in 1988 Wells Fargo

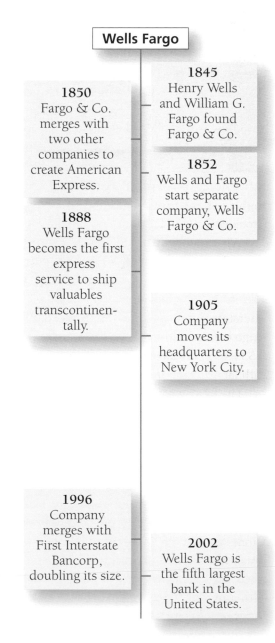

Wells Fargo

1845
Henry Wells and William G. Fargo found Fargo & Co.

1850
Fargo & Co. merges with two other companies to create American Express.

1852
Wells and Fargo start separate company, Wells Fargo & Co.

1888
Wells Fargo becomes the first express service to ship valuables transcontinentally.

1905
Company moves its headquarters to New York City.

1996
Company merges with First Interstate Bancorp, doubling its size.

2002
Wells Fargo is the fifth largest bank in the United States.

enabled these advances at the time of the Crocker merger.

With a growing reputation in the banking industry, Wells Fargo acquired more banks in 1990 and the company doubled in size in 1996, when it merged with First Interstate Bancorp. Two years later Wells Fargo merged with Norwest of Minneapolis, a $34 billion merger that created the seventh largest bank in the country.

The Norwest–Wells Fargo merger brought in an era of heavy branding known internally as the Next Stage. The stagecoach and horses had become Wells Fargo's primary logo in the mid-1960s. As Norwest gave up its own logo in the merger, Wells Fargo introduced its image and its history to former Norwest customers throughout Minnesota and the Midwest. The campaign, which lasted through September 2000, targeted each state with advertisements rich with images of the Old West. In major Norwest areas like Minneapolis, Wells Fargo even brought out the Stagecoach Appearance program—a team of horses and a Concord coach—and erected Wells Fargo history museums.

In July 2002 Wells Fargo celebrated its 150th anniversary, with stagecoaches taking to the streets in San Francisco, New York, and Los Angeles, and the CEO, Dick Kovacevich, ringing the closing bell of the New York Stock Exchange. Wells Fargo had more than $308 billion in assets and 5,400 branches in the United States alone.

CEO Carl Reichardt at Wells Fargo's San Francisco office in 1987.

Further Reading

Beebe, Lucius, and Charles Clegg. *U.S. West: The Saga of Wells Fargo.* New York: E. P. Dutton, 1949.

Fradkin, Philip L. *Stagecoach.* New York: Simon & Schuster Source, 2002.

Winther, Oscar Osburn. *Express and Stagecoach: Days in California, from the Gold Rush to the Civil War.* London: Oxford University Press, 1936.

—*Laura Lambert*

See also:
Amazon.com; E-Business;
Internet; Yahoo!

Whitman, Meg

1957–
President of eBay

One of Silicon Valley's highest-profile women, Margaret "Meg" Whitman, is the president and chief executive officer of America's most successful Internet company, eBay. Under Whitman's leadership, the online auction site has evolved into the world's largest personal online trading company. As of 2002 eBay had more than 12 million items for sale on any given day.

The company was founded in 1995 by Pierre Omidyar as an online venue for trading Pez candy dispensers. The Web site is basically an online marketplace: sellers use the eBay site to offer items for sale by auction and pay eBay a listing fee for this service. In essence, eBay is a go-between: it does not handle inventory, distribution, or returns; rather, its focus is connecting buyers and sellers. Handling 79 million transactions per quarter, from stuffed animals to private jets, eBay so far appears to be fulfilling its mission of "helping people trade practically anything on earth."

Whitman already had an impressive resume before she joined eBay: a degree in economics from Princeton University (1977), a master's in business administration from Harvard Business School (1979), brand management training at Procter and Gamble, and marketing and consulting experience at blue-chip companies, including Bain and Company, Walt Disney, and Stride-Rite. In 1997, when eBay first recruited Whitman for the CEO position, she was the general manager of the Playskool Division of Hasbro, one of the country's biggest manufacturers of toys, games, and puzzles. At first Whitman was not particularly interested in working for a little-known dot-com whose content seemed to consist of electronic classifieds. It was only the reputation and the persistence of the head-hunter that persuaded her to fly to San Jose, California, to view the day-to-day operations.

Upon visiting the company, Whitman immediately recognized that eBay took unique advantage of the Internet's ability to simultaneously connect thousands of users every single day all over the world. She listened to Omidyar's stories of people meeting and connecting over shared areas of interest and heard testimonials of people whose daily habits now included the furtive monitoring of their auctions. She saw the ingredients for the making of a great brand. Unlike Internet companies like Amazon.com, which provide services similar to—albeit perhaps more efficiently than—many existing companies, eBay enabled people to do something they could never do before. Impressed by eBay's potential as well as its compound monthly growth rate, Whitman and her family took the risk and moved to the West Coast in February 1998.

Whitman immediately set about improving eBay's corporate image. She created its first national advertising strategy; modified the Web site and logo with eye-catching colors and design elements; and hired senior staff with marketing experience. Whitman also

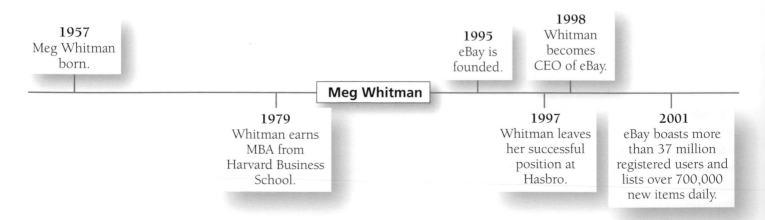

1957
Meg Whitman born.

1979
Whitman earns MBA from Harvard Business School.

Meg Whitman

1995
eBay is founded.

1997
Whitman leaves her successful position at Hasbro.

1998
Whitman becomes CEO of eBay.

2001
eBay boasts more than 37 million registered users and lists over 700,000 new items daily.

Meg Whitman outside eBay headquarters in San Jose, California, in 2001.

placed immediate emphasis on profitability, contrary to the many dot-com ventures that initially emphasized sales volume over profits.

Whitman believes that eBay's long-term success depends on enabling its users to build successful businesses on eBay's Web site. She views the company's main task as providing an efficient, safe, and vibrant marketplace for the community, which she refers to as eBay's "army of entrepreneurs."

To date Whitman has improved eBay's marketplace in a variety of ways. To protect users against fraudulent activity, Whitman created a trust and safety policy underwritten by Lloyds of London. To increase eBay's size and visibility, she encouraged established companies to sell on eBay's Web site and also formed strategic marketing alliances with IBM and would-be competitor AOL. By closely following the trading habits of eBay's users, Whitman has identified and adopted innovations that have broadened the scope of eBay's marketplace. For example, she allowed sellers offering multiple items to create customized online storefronts. Whitman also expanded eBay's auction categories by introducing eBay Premier, which includes high-priced items from leading auction houses and antiques dealers, as well as eBay Professional Services, which allows eBay users to offer and purchase various professional services, for example, freelance Web design, accounting, and software development. To appeal to customers who favor fixed-price offerings over auctions, Whitman created a fixed-price sales channel by acquiring the low-price Internet retailer, Half.com. Finally, Whitman has strengthened eBay's international presence by creating a multitude of other country-specific sites and by adopting automatic translation and currency conversion functions, which serve to facilitate international transactions.

Despite owning hundreds of millions of dollars worth of eBay stock, Whitman continues to work in a cubicle, dress casually, and correspond directly with eBay users. Her unassuming, down-to-earth manner and conservative "penny-pinching" business approach are not the only things that set her apart from most dot-com CEOs. Most important, she has managed to developed one of the few Internet businesses whose success can already be measured in positive cash flow and profits.

Further Reading

Batistick, Mike. "Meg Whitman." *Current Biography* (February 2000): 86–91.

Cohen, Adam. *The Perfect Store: Inside eBay*. Boston: Little, Brown, 2002.

Roth, Daniel. "Meg Muscles eBay Uptown." *Fortune*, July 5, 1999, 81–86.

—*Christina Campbell*

Winfrey, Oprah

1954–
Media entrepreneur

Although she is most famous for her feel-good talk show, Oprah Winfrey is one of the most successful businesswomen in the United States. In addition to starting her own media company, she shook the foundations of the publishing industry with her on-air book club.

Winfrey was born on January 29, 1954, in Kosciusko, Mississippi. Her mother, Vernita Lee, unmarried and not involved with Vernon Winfrey, the man she named as Oprah's father, desperately needed employment. She left Mississippi for the North, turning the care of her baby over to her mother, Hattie Mae Lee. Hattie Mae was a paradox. She brutalized Winfrey with daily whippings to instill good behavior and at the same time tutored Winfrey academically. Winfrey was a quick learner and, at the age of three, was able to read, write, do math, and recite. Her speaking performances at church brought her acclaim and her academic skills brought admiration from her teachers. Perhaps because of her success, Winfrey was shunned by her classmates. She recalls taking solace in books.

While still in elementary school, Winfrey was shuttled off to Milwaukee, Wisconsin, to live with her mother. Now responsible for two younger siblings while her mother worked away from home,

Winfrey faced new hardships. In school, however, she continued to achieve at a high level, and in 1968, at age 14, she obtained a scholarship to a high school in suburban Fox Point, where she was the only black in a student body of about 2,000. She was warmly welcomed by her new classmates. Invited to their homes, she observed life from a different perspective. From their advantaged economic position, the suburban families were able to focus on the importance of learning for their children and to encourage them to plan for college and professional careers.

The long ride home from school at night—requiring three bus transfers—returned Winfrey to a different environment. Squeezed into the noisy city quarters she shared with her mother, a stepbrother, a stepsister, and an assortment of men who came and went, Winfrey became frightened, then frustrated, then downright rebellious. At the point when Winfrey was no longer controllable, Vernita contacted Vernon Winfrey in Nashville, Tennessee, and he and his wife, Zelma, agreed to take Winfrey into their home.

In Nashville Winfrey suffered no abuse, but Vernon and Zelma maintained extremely high standards for her. Vernon disciplined with lectures, insisting on chaste behavior and high grades. Zelma demanded that Winfrey read and turn in book reports for five books every two weeks; she also expected Winfrey to learn 20 new words each week. Winfrey thrived. Her high school grades were excellent, and she was

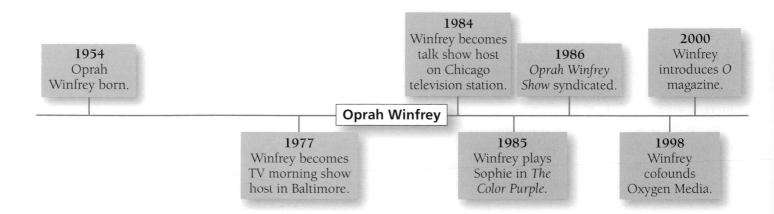

1954
Oprah Winfrey born.

1977
Winfrey becomes TV morning show host in Baltimore.

1984
Winfrey becomes talk show host on Chicago television station.

1985
Winfrey plays Sophie in *The Color Purple.*

1986
Oprah Winfrey Show syndicated.

1998
Winfrey cofounds Oxygen Media.

2000
Winfrey introduces *O* magazine.

Oprah Winfrey

enthusiastic about her classes, especially those in theater arts and speech.

After high school Winfrey set off for college. She lasted only a short time, leaving to take a television job in Nashville. As a vibrant, well-read, and personable young woman, Winfrey was well suited to work in television. When she was 22 she left Nashville and her father and stepmother, striking out on her own for Baltimore, Maryland. There she also worked in television, initially as a news reporter, a job not as well suited to her personality as the morning spot she landed in 1977. As she interviewed guests and interacted with the audience, local ratings skyrocketed, surpassing even those of nationally syndicated talk show host, Phil Donahue.

In 1984 Winfrey got a break that moved her to the city she has called home ever since. A Chicago television executive found himself urgently in need of a talk show host; his assistant, who had worked with Winfrey, showed him films of Winfrey's Baltimore morning show. The producer was entranced, as were his associates, so they flew Winfrey to Chicago and she signed immediately.

Winfrey continued to follow the Donahue format, tackling tough, women-oriented issues (home viewers at that time were mostly women) and fielding questions from the studio audience. She was a smash hit, once again topping Donahue's ratings. In time, Winfrey became the number-one talk show host in the nation and the highest-paid black woman in America. She owed her success to more than her interviewing skills, which some critics have found lacking. Her guests have described the mood of comfort she generated through her expressions of empathy, genuine curiosity, and good humor. This mood, they have reported, put them at ease and enabled them to speak candidly on her show about matters of deep personal importance.

At age 31 Winfrey received what she considers her highest honor. Movie producer Steven Spielberg cast her as Sophie in his movie *The Color Purple* (1985). Because Winfrey had remained an impassioned reader

since childhood, she knew and identified with the character. Her portrayal won her an Academy Award nomination.

In 1986 *The Oprah Winfrey Show* was syndicated to television stations throughout the United States, beginning Winfrey's climb to financial and popular superstardom. Winfrey's monthly book club, a regular feature on her talk show from 1996 to 2002, became the nation's best-known guide to pleasure reading and book buying. Publishers coveted the Winfrey stamp of approval; any book discussed on her show was virtually guaranteed to be a major best-seller.

In 1998 Winfrey cofounded Oxygen Media to produce her show, becoming the

Winfrey and former South African president Nelson Mandela at a December 2002 ceremony marking the start of construction of the Oprah Winfrey Leadership Academy for Girls in Johannesburg, South Africa.

third woman in history to own her own entertainment production company. In 2000 Oxygen Media launched a cable television channel, and Winfrey premiered her highly successful magazine, *O*. In 2003 *Forbes* magazine included Winfrey on its annual billionaire's list: Winfrey is the first African American woman to become a billionaire.

Winfrey has won 33 Emmy awards for excellence in television broadcasting and was named one of the twentieth century's most influential people by *Time* magazine. In efforts to explain Winfrey's success, some observers have emphasized her on-air persona, including her attractive appearance, her snappy personality, and her capacity for empathy. Others have emphasized her intellectual qualities, along with her inner strength and self-confidence. These factors are no doubt relevant, but success of the kind Winfrey has attained is exceptional even among people known to be engaging, strong, and intelligent—her achievements also reflect exceptional entrepreneurial drive and business acumen.

Further Reading

Lowe, Janet. *Oprah Winfrey Speaks: Insights from the World's Most Influential Voice*. New York: John Wiley & Sons, 2001.
Waldron, Robert. *Oprah!* New York: St. Martin's Press, 1991.

—*Karen Ehrle*

Women in the Workforce

Throughout history women have always worked, but much of that work was confined to the home and farm. Women now have more job opportunities than ever before, although a number of inequalities remain in the workforce.

Working outside the Home

Prior to industrialization, women primarily worked on farms or from home, assembling products like shoes and clothes one at a time as piecework. Some women worked inside others' homes as domestic servants. Not until industrialization did women begin to seek work outside the home in large numbers.

The new factories were willing to hire women because they would work for lower wages than would men. Women, especially poor, unmarried women and immigrants, had few job options available to them. When they went to work in the mills and garment industries, women had to settle for whatever pay they could get, often very little. For example, in 1845 women working in the cotton mills of Pittsburgh and Allegheny City, Pennsylvania, received $2.50 for working a 72-hour week.

Although women did agitate and go on strike for better wages, early trade unions were primarily concerned with keeping women out of the workforce. In 1867 William H. Sylvis, one of the founders of the National Labor Union, began pressing for the admission of women into the trade unions, but most men regarded women as a menace that drove wages down by taking underpaid jobs when they should have stayed at home.

Low wages, poor working conditions, and few or no rights characterized women's experience of the workforce into the twentieth century. In 1910 women made up 20 percent of the American workforce, and individual women earned an average of $6 a week while men earned an average of $15 a week.

New Opportunities

World War I brought opportunities for women to move into new areas of employment. Vacancies left by men gone to war, in office work and in some new professional fields, were filled by women. At the same time, the social status of women was changing. More women were going to school and to college. More people lived in cities, where women had greater opportunities for work outside the farm and the home. New political concepts like socialism and progressive reform argued for more-equal treatment.

The Roaring Twenties, a period of social permissiveness following the end of World War I, broke down social barriers for middle-class women and opened new professional fields. Nevertheless, women's pay continued to lag far behind that of men. In the 1920s, few would have argued that women deserved to be paid the same as men. Most women left the workplace when they married and had children.

In 1919 the first equal pay laws were enacted in the United States, but only 24 states required women who did the same or comparable work as men to be paid equally. During the Great Depression, women were almost always the first to be laid off.

World War II again brought labor shortages in many fields. The production demands of the war drew large numbers of women into the workforce: over 250,000

A woodcut from the sixteenth century depicts women working at a mountain mine, where they cut ore from pieces of rock.

The more WOMEN at work the sooner we WIN!

WOMEN ARE NEEDED ALSO AS:

FARM WORKERS	WAITRESSES	TIMEKEEPERS	LAUNDRESSES
TYPISTS	BUS DRIVERS	ELEVATOR OPERATORS	TEACHERS
SALESPEOPLE	TAXI DRIVERS	MESSENGERS	CONDUCTORS

— and in hundreds of other war jobs!

SEE YOUR LOCAL U.S. EMPLOYMENT SERVICE

OWI Poster No. 59. Additional copies may be obtained upon request from the Division of Public Inquiries, Office of War Information, Washington, D.C.

A recruiting poster from World War II encourages women to contribute to the war effort by taking a job.

Because of the large number of American women taking jobs in the war industries during World War II, the National War Labor Board urged employers in 1942 to voluntarily raise women's wages to make them comparable to men's. Most employers did not heed this request, and at the war's end most women lost their new jobs to make room for returning veterans.

After the war, many women dedicated themselves to raising families, but some did keep their jobs. Wartime experience had proved that women were capable of performing many jobs previously reserved for men. In the 1950s many women were persuaded by the highly consumerist attitudes prevalent at the time to return to the workforce. However, 95 percent of working women were confined to a female job ghetto of light manufacturing, retail sales, clerical work, health, and education.

Even within these fields, women often received low pay and were subject to harassment and arbitrary treatment. Few legal avenues for complaint were available to women, and a slap on the backside or a grope in the office corridor were often considered the prerogatives of being a male boss.

Equal Pay for Equal Work

Although women had proven they could work in many fields, they still faced barriers to equal pay and equal treatment in almost every field. Until the early 1960s newspapers published separate job listings for men and women. Jobs were categorized according to sex, with the management and higher paid jobs listed almost exclusively under "Help Wanted—Male." In some cases the ads ran identical jobs under male and female listings—but with separate pay scales. Not until the passage of the Equal Pay Act on June 10, 1963, did paying women lower rates for the same job become illegal.

The act was gradually expanded over the next decade. In 1970 the U.S. Court of Appeals for the Third Circuit ruled, in *Schultz v. Wheaton Glass Company*, that employers could no longer simply change the job titles of women workers in an attempt to justify

women entered the armed forces; 500,000 women found jobs building aircraft; the metal, chemical, and rubber industries saw a 460 percent increase in women workers; 10 percent of shipyard workers were female, although virtually no women had been employed in that industry before the attack on Pearl Harbor. The number of women in trade unions quadrupled, and the image of Rosie the Riveter became a national icon as women entered fields that were previously closed to them.

paying them less than men. In 1974 the U.S. Supreme Court ruled in *Corning Glass Works v. Brennan* that a wage difference occurring "simply because men would not work at the low rates paid women" was unacceptable. These cases exposed wage discrimination in the workforce but did not end it.

Between 1950 and 1960 women with full-time jobs earned on average between 59–64 cents for every dollar their male counterparts earned in the same job. In 1997 women earned 74 percent of men's wages—an improvement of less than half a cent a year. The gap is gradually closing, especially for college-educated women, but wages are not the only barriers women face in the workforce.

Problems in the Workplace

Gradually women have won the rights to equal pay and to be free from sexual harassment in the workplace. Although women are no longer restricted to a female job ghetto, many careers are still only partly open to women. Discrimination against women is still legal for jobs that are hazardous or dangerous; most trade jobs, painting and construction, for example, are controlled by male-dominated unions and remain effectively closed to women. However, the greatest bar facing women in the workforce is the issue of children and child care.

Assuming that women will eventually take time off to have children, many companies place women in a much slower promotional track than men, dubbed the "mommy track," where opportunities for advancement are few. Although companies can no longer legally deny women promotion on the basis of sex, women frequently find they are simply not promoted above a certain level—what has been called the "glass ceiling."

Women's rights advocates point out that both the glass ceiling and mommy track are vicious cycles. They relegate women to lower-paid positions, so that when a couple does decide to have children, the woman's lower income can more easily be spared, and thus the woman is the one selected to give up her job. Women must often choose between

career and family when they would like both. For poor women and single mothers, the problems can be even worse. Child care is expensive, and very few companies pay for day care or offer on-site day care, which would allow working parents to spend time with their children during the day. In most other Western countries the government either provides or subsidizes child care rather than leaving it entirely to the private sector.

Women in Selected Occupations 1975 to 2000 (percent of total employed)			
Occupation	Year		
	1975	1985	2000
Auto mechanic	0.5	0.6	1.2
Bartender	35.2	47.9	51.8
Brick masons and stonemasons	NA	NA	0.7
Bus driver	37.7	49.2	49.6
Butchers and meat cutters	NA	NA	27.3
Cab driver, chauffeur	8.7	10.9	10.8
Childcare worker	98.4	96.1	97.5
Cleaners and servants	NA	NA	94.8
Computer programmer	25.6	34.3	26.5
Computer systems analyst	14.8	28.0	29.2
Data entry keyer	92.8	90.7	83.5
Data processing equipment repairer	1.8	10.4	15.4
Dental assistant	100.0	99.0	96.4
Dentist	1.8	6.5	18.7
Dietitian	NA	NA	89.9
Drywall installers	NA	NA	5.6
Economist	13.1	34.5	53.3
Editor, reporter	44.6	51.7	55.8
Firefighter	NA	NA	3.0
Lawyer, judge	7.1	18.2	29.7
Librarian	81.1	87.0	85.2
Mail carrier (postal service)	8.7	17.2	30.6
Physician	13.0	17.2	27.9
Police officer, detective (public service)	NA	NA	14.2
Registered nurse	97.0	95.1	92.8
Social worker	60.8	66.7	72.4
Teacher, elementary school	85.4	84.4	83.3
Telephone installer, repairer	4.8	12.8	13.1
Telephone operator	93.3	88.8	83.9
Waiter	91.1	84.0	76.7
Welder	4.4	4.8	4.9

Note: NA = Not available.
Source: U.S. Department of Labor, Bureau of Labor Statistics, *Employment and Earnings*, January issues, 1975 to 2000.

Employment of Women by Marital Status and Age of Children
1970 to 2000

	Total			Children under 6			Children 6 to 17		
	Single	Married[1]	Other[2]	Single	Married[1]	Other[2]	Single	Married[1]	Other[2]
In labor force (in millions)									
1970	7.0	18.4	5.9	NA	3.9	0.6	NA	6.3	1.3
1980	11.2	24.9	8.8	0.3	5.2	1.0	0.2	8.4	2.6
1985	12.9	27.7	10.3	0.7	6.4	1.1	0.4	8.5	2.9
1990	14.0	31.0	11.2	0.9	7.2	1.2	0.6	9.3	3.0
1995	15.0	33.6	12.0	1.3	7.8	1.3	0.8	10.2	3.3
2000	17.8	35.0	13.2	1.8	7.3	1.1	1.2	10.8	3.4
Participation rate (in percent)									
1970	53.0	40.8	39.1	NA	30.3	52.2	NA	49.2	66.9
1980	61.5	50.1	44.0	44.1	45.1	60.3	67.6	61.7	74.6
1985	65.2	54.2	45.6	46.5	53.4	59.7	64.1	67.8	77.8
1990	66.4	58.2	46.8	48.7	58.9	63.6	69.7	73.6	79.7
1995	65.5	61.1	47.3	53.0	63.5	66.3	67.0	76.2	79.5
2000	68.6	62.0	50.2	70.5	62.7	76.6	79.7	77.2	85.0

Note: NA = Not available.
[1]Husband present. [2]Widowed, divorced, or separated.
Source: U.S. Department of Labor, Bureau of Labor Statistics, *Employment and Earnings*, January issues, 1970–2000.

These nations have higher participation rates of women in the labor force.

Women still bear the major responsibility of the home. A 1968 survey found that, on average, husbands spent just over 2 hours a week on housework (not including child care), compared with 39 hours a week for wives. By 1991 surveys found husbands spending about 7 hours a week on housework, compared with 25 hours for wives.

Another problem women face in the workplace is sexual harassment. Until the 1980s a woman could do little to avoid sexual harassment except quit her job. Laws are now on the books to prevent sexual harassment, and women can sue for compensation. Harassment, however, can take an insidious form, consisting of veiled comments, jokes, and offensive stories that create a climate of fear or discomfort. Attempts to control this kind of behavior with more laws and workplace rules have led many to argue that feminists have gone overboard by creating a situation in which a harmless joke can end in a lawsuit.

Women have gained independence, dignity, respect, greater bargaining power at home, freedom, and the ability to socialize and have a life apart from family by entering the workforce. The gap in labor force participation rates and in earnings has narrowed. Occupational segregation and hours of housework have decreased, improving the ability of women, especially college-educated women, to combine career with family. This record of success has lots of qualifications, however. Few women actually achieve a high level of success at both career and family; the earning power for some minority women has actually declined since 1980. Past progress points in a new direction for future improvements—to the day when both men and women can choose exactly what they want to do.

Further Reading

Coplon, Jennifer Kane. *Single Older Women in the Workforce: By Necessity, or Choice?* New York: Garland Publishing, 1997.

Friedan, Betty. *Beyond Gender: The New Politics of Work and Family*. Baltimore, Md.: Johns Hopkins University Press, 1997.

Gourley, Catherine. *Good Girl Work: Factories, Sweatshops, and How Women Changed Their Role in the American Workforce*. Brookfield, Conn.: Millbrook Press, 1999.

Weiss, Ann E. *The Glass Ceiling: A Look at Women in the Workforce*. Brookfield, Conn.: Twenty First Century Books, 1999.

—Lisa Magloff

Working Conditions

Working conditions is a blanket term for a wide variety of on-the-job concerns, including worker safety, hours, benefits, and discrimination. Although the earliest laborers in the United States often had no more rights and protections than did slaves, centuries of labor struggle have produced a body of federal laws that set a minimum wage, protect against environmental health hazards, and prohibit employment discrimination based on age, race, and sex. Strides have been made to address the needs of workers in many hazardous industries, for example, mining; however, in other industries, for example, the garment industry, abuses are still rampant. The global economy has brought to light the disparity in working conditions across the globe and within numerous industries.

Industrialization

As cities and opportunities grew during the colonial period, workers, including shoemakers and printers, formed guilds and other organizations to regulate and protect their professions. In 1786 printers in Philadelphia walked out to protest a wage reduction, in what is often cited as the first successful strike in the United States; the printers won a $6 per week minimum wage. Although the rights of skilled labor seemed to advance somewhat during this era, factory workers still faced grueling circumstances and low wages.

At the beginning of the nineteenth century, girls who left home for the mills faced somewhat less harsh conditions. After the first factory opened in Lowell, Massachusetts, in 1823, girls and young women from the ages of 10 to 30 flocked to the area, drawn by promises of cash wages, room, and board. Although the Lowell mills paid their workers relatively fair wages, the days were long—often 14 hours during the week—and the living conditions were restrictive—curfews, codes of conduct, and rules about the Sabbath and temperance. Most women lasted less than a year.

In 1828 mill workers in Dover, New Hampshire, called a strike against working conditions that included a 12.5-cent fine for tardiness and a ban on talking on the job. Workers in the textile industry, including the Lowell mill girls, called strikes throughout the 1830s and 1840s. One of the recurring demands during this era was for the 10-hour day.

By 1840 both Presidents Andrew Jackson and Martin Van Buren had come out in support of the 10-hour workday. In 1843 Connecticut and Massachusetts became the first two states to limit children's workdays to 10 hours. Five years later, New Hampshire became the first state to extend the law to all workers. By the 1850s the 8-hour movement had already begun. The U.S. government instated the 8-hour day for federal laborers in 1868.

See also:
Fair Labor Standards Act;
Globalization; Lowell Mills;
Occupational Safety and
Health Administration;
Temporary Workers.

The Physical Condition of England's Textile Workers

Any man who has stood at twelve o'clock at the single narrow doorway, which serves as the place of exit for the hands employed in the great cotton-mills, must acknowledge that an uglier set of men and women, of boys and girls, taking them in the mass, it would be impossible to congregate in a smaller compass. Their complexion is sallow and pallid—with a peculiar flatness of feature, caused by the want of a proper quantity of adipose substance to cushion out the cheeks. Their stature low—the average height of four hundred men, measured at different times, and different places, being five feet six inches. Their limbs slender, and playing badly and ungracefully. A very general bowing of the legs. Great numbers of girls and women walking lamely or awkwardly, with raised chests and spinal flexures. Nearly all have flat feet, accompanied with a down-tread, differing very widely from the elasticity of action in the foot and ankle, attendant upon perfect formation. Hair thin and straight—many of the men having but little beard, and that in patches of a few hairs, much resembling its growth among the red men of America. A spiritless and dejected air, a sprawling and wide action of the legs, and an appearance, taken as a whole, giving the world but "little assurance of a man," or if so, "most sadly cheated of his fair proportions . . . ."

Factory labour is a species of work, in some respects singularly unfitted for children. Cooped up in a heated atmosphere, debarred the necessary exercise, remaining in one position for a series of hours, one set or system of muscles alone called into activity, it cannot be wondered at—that its effects are injurious to the physical growth of a child. Where the bony system is still imperfect, the vertical position it is compelled to retain, influences its direction; the spinal column bends beneath the weight of the head, bulges out laterally, or is dragged forward by the weight of the parts composing the chest, the pelvis yields beneath the opposing pressure downwards, and the resistance given by the thigh-bones; its capacity is lessened, sometimes more and sometimes less; the legs curve, and the whole body loses height, in consequence of this general yielding and bending of its parts.

—P. Gaskell, *The Manufacturing Population of England*, 1833, The Victorian Web, West Virginia University, http://65.107.211.206/history/workers2.html (March 20, 2003)

Family members arrive at the New York City morgue to identify the bodies of victims of the Triangle Shirtwaist Fire that killed 146 factory workers, mainly young immigrant women, in 1911.

Twentieth-Century Working Conditions

Although certain improvements in working conditions were being made on a government level, economic hardship and an influx of immigrants kept wages down and hours up in many industries across the country, especially in cities. The latter half of the nineteenth century and early decades of the twentieth century saw the rapid growth of factory and tenement sweatshops. The dangers of sweatshops—overcrowding, lack of ventilation, unsafe structures, and the usual long hours and low pay—were brought to national attention in 1911. In March of that year, 146 workers, mostly young female immigrants, perished in a fire at the Triangle Shirtwaist factory in New York City, primarily because the only exit doors for the sweatshop had been locked from the outside. In response to the public outcry about safety in sweatshops, New York City created the Factory Investigating Commission.

The early twentieth century was marked by a wave of government activity to improve conditions for working Americans. In his last hours as president in 1913, President William Howard Taft signed the bill that created the U.S. Department of Labor. A rush of labor-related acts quickly followed, including the La Follette Seaman's Act (1915), which regulated the working conditions of seamen, and the Adamson Act (1916), which established an 8-hour day for railroad workers. In 1936 the Walsh–Healy Act established guidelines for minimum wages and safety standards for all federal contracts. Two years later, the Fair Labor Standards Act (FLSA) expanded those rights and benefits to all workers, establishing a 25¢/hour minimum wage, with time-and-a-half overtime pay for each hour over 40 worked per week. (A 1949 amendment to the FLSA directly prohibited child labor for the first time.)

In keeping with the times, legislation of the 1960s focused on workers' rights, as well as a less tangible aspect of working conditions—discrimination. The Equal Pay Act of 1963 prohibited wage differences for workers based on sex; the Civil Rights Act of 1964 prohibited discrimination based on race, sex, religion, or national origin; and the Age Discrimination in Employment Act of 1968 prohibited age discrimination, making it illegal to fire someone aged 40–65 solely based on age. At the same time, occupational injuries and deaths were on the rise. In response, the Occupational Safety and Health Administration (OSHA) was created in 1971 to improve safety and protect workers from work-related death, illness, and injury. OSHA addresses decidedly modern work issues as well, providing ergonomic guidelines for office workers and computer users and testing of blood-borne pathogen levels for medical workers.

Key Legislation Affecting Working Conditions

La Follette Seaman's Act (1915): Regulated working conditions of seamen

Adamson Act (1916): Established 8-hour day for railroad workers

Welsh–Healy Act (1936): Established guidelines for minimum wages and safety standards for all federal contracts

Fair Labor Standards Act (1938): Established minimum wage and maximum workweek for all workers; forbade labor by children under 16; restricted to nonhazardous occupations those under 18

Equal Pay Act (1963): Prohibited wage differences for workers based on sex

Civil Rights Act (1964): Prohibited discrimination based on race, religion, sex, or national origin

Age Discrimination in Employment Act (1968): Prohibited age discrimination, making illegal the firing of someone 40 to 65 years old based solely on age

Fatal Occupational Injuries in the United States: By Industry and Event 2000

	Fatalities	Event (percent distribution)					Rate (per 100,000 employees)
		Transportation incidents	Assaults and violent acts	Contact with harmful objects or equipment	Falls	Exposure to harmful materials or environments	
Agriculture, forestry, fishing	720	51	7	25	9	8	21
Mining	156	30	ND	37	12	8	30
Coal mining	40	35	ND	43	ND	ND	53
Oil and gas extraction	83	30	ND	30	12	8	27
General building contractors	175	14	7	18	43	12	ND
Heavy construction, except building	284	44	ND	28	7	17	ND
Special trade contractors	672	20	4	19	4	15	ND
Lumber and wood products	186	31	3	57	ND	5	24
Local passenger transit	84	42	55	ND	ND	ND	15
Trucking and warehousing	566	80	4	9	4	2	21
Transportation by air	97	84	ND	10	ND	ND	11
Electric, gas, sanitary services	84	54	ND	13	ND	18	8
Automotive dealer and service stations	95	41	43	ND	ND	ND	4
Auto repair, services, and parking	132	28	30	24	ND	ND	8
Food manufacturing	68	37	ND	31	9	15	4
Food stores	145	10	86	ND	ND	ND	4
Eating and drinking places	138	13	73	ND	9	ND	2
Finance, insurance, real estate	79	41	33	6	13	8	1
Business services	199	45	20	8	15	10	2
Government	571	58	21	8	5	5	3
Total	5,915	44	16	17	12	8	4

Note: ND = No data reported.
Source: U.S. Bureau of Labor Statistics, USDL News, 01-261, August 14, 2001.

Contemporary Issues in Working Conditions

Although ergonomics may seem a far cry from earlier demands for a 10-hour work-day, many of the earliest concerns about working conditions still exist. In 1995, 72 illegal Thai immigrants were found in a series of apartment–factories in El Monte, California, sewing in near-captivity. The discovery merely highlighted the growing

A factory worker pours liquid into molds at one of Tijuana, Mexico's many maquiladora plants, which were built because of the need for cheap Mexican labor by U.S. industries.

serious violation of health and safety laws. Similar concerns exist for the thousands of other workers in the United States, for example, day laborers and migrant farm workers, who work without the benefits and protections of unions.

Some white-collar jobs, especially in the technology industry, have also been criticized as sweatshops. During the early days of high technology and the Internet boom, many workers did not question—and even embraced—the 24/7 workweek, with cell phones, beepers, laptops, and telecommuting enabling constant access and contact. In many companies, 10-hour days and six-day weeks again became the norm. This time, however, workers often committed themselves to such schedules, driven both by the heady excitement of the new industry and, especially for middle-aged workers, by the fear of being replaced.

Outside the tech industry, the boundaries of a 9-to-5 workday also dissolved during the economic boom times of the 1980s and 1990s. At the same time, in many sectors, standard employee benefits—paid vacation and health and dental insurance—started to disappear. Low- to mid-level corporate employees—generally office and administrative assistants—were often replaced by a temporary workforce that tolled without paid sick days or guarantee of employment, and with little to no hope of advancement.

concern about exploited manual labor, from Mexico's maquiladoras—predominantly U.S.-owned assembly plants along the U.S.–Mexico border—to sweatshops in Malaysia. As corporations relocate facilities to countries with the lowest production costs, critics decry a "race to the bottom" where, to be competitive, countries with already substandard working conditions are forced to cut wages and increase hours, pushing working conditions lower and lower across the globe.

The health and safety standards in many of these offshore factories are unregulated and dangerously low. Even within the United States, the Department of Labor estimated in 1996 that nearly half of the country's 22,000 garment shops were in

Further Reading

Fraser, Jill Andresky. *White-Collar Sweatshop: The Deterioration of Work and Its Rewards in Corporate America.* New York: W. W. Norton, 2001.

Kamel, Rachel, and Anya Hoffman, eds. *The Maquiladora Reader: Cross-Border Organizing since NAFTA.* Philadelphia: American Friends Service Committee, 1999.

Lewis, Sinclair. *Cheap and Contented Labor: The Picture of a Southern Mill Town in 1929.* New York: United Textile Workers of America and Women's Trade Union League, 1929.

Robinson, Harriet H. *Loom and Spindle: Or, Life Among the Early Mill Girls.* 1898. Reprint, Kailua, Hawaii: Press Pacifica, 1976.

—*Laura Lambert*

World Bank

The World Bank is a group of organizations based in Washington, D.C., that is funded by the international community and lends money to countries for economic development. Originally known as the International Bank for Reconstruction and Development (IBRD), it was established in 1944 to provide loans for postwar economic regeneration. More recently, the World Bank has concentrated on providing both economic and technical assistance to developing countries, with an increasing focus on relieving global poverty.

The Creation of the World Bank

Along with its sister organization the International Monetary Fund (IMF), the IBRD was created at the United Nations Monetary and Financial Conference held at Bretton Woods, New Hampshire, in July 1944. On the premise that "it is in the interest of all nations that postwar reconstruction should be rapid . . . [to] . . . aid political stability and foster peace," the conference proposed the establishment of a new international organization that could both increase the amount and share the risks of foreign investment. The IBRD would "assist in providing capital through normal channels at reasonable rates of interest and for long periods for projects which will raise the productivity of the borrowing country."

After commencing operations in June 1946, the IBRD made its first loans to help with postwar reconstruction. Within three years, the focus of its activities had shifted subtly and the bank began to concentrate on providing funds to help poorer countries with more general economic development. This also brought a shift in the territory of its operations from the nations of Western Europe, which had sought economic help with rebuilding their war-torn industries and economies, to the developing nations of Africa, Asia, and Latin America.

Since that time, the World Bank (still formally known as IBRD) has created a number

World Bank

1944
The International Bank for Reconstruction and Development created.

1946
Bank makes first loans to help with postwar reconstruction.

1955
Bank forms Economic Development Institute to provide technical assistance to member countries.

1956
Bank establishes International Finance Corporation to promote private investment in developing countries.

1962
Bank creates International Development Association to provide long-term loans to debtor nations.

1966
International Center for Settlement of Investment Disputes formed to resolve disagreements between governments and private foreign companies.

1988
Multilateral Investment Guarantee Agency formed to encourage internal investment by developing nations.

1993
World Bank withdraws from financing dam on India's Narmada River due to environmental protests.

2002
World Bank has 184 members and provides developing nations with a total of $19 billion in loans.

See also:
Asian Development Bank; Globalization; International Monetary Fund; World Trade Organization.

of related institutions to help advance different aspects of its work. In 1955 the bank's Economic Development Institute (EDI) was formed to provide technical assistance to member countries. In 1956 the bank established its International Finance Corporation (IFC) to promote private investment in developing countries. In 1962 the bank created the International Development Association (IDA) to provide long-term loans to nations that are heavily in debt. In October 1966 another World Bank institution, the International Center for Settlement of Investment Disputes (ICSID), was formed to resolve disagreements (for example, when governments try to nationalize a company's assets) between member governments and private foreign companies that invest in their countries. The bank's most recent offshoot, the Multilateral Investment Guarantee Agency (MIGA), was formed in 1988 to encourage internal investment by developing nations by offering guarantees against the risks involved. Collectively, the IBRD, IFC, IDA, ICSID, and MIGA are known as the World Bank Group.

The bank is controlled by its members through a board of governors and executive directors. Members appoint the governors, who meet once a year. The governors, in turn, control the board of 21 executive directors who are responsible for determining the bank's policies and approving loans. Five directors are appointed by the bank's largest shareholders; the remainder are elected by the governors. Overall control of the bank rests with its president, who is by tradition appointed for a five-year term by the United States—the bank's largest shareholder. Although the IBRD, the IFC, and the IDA are separate institutions, considerable overlap exists among them: only World Bank members can join the IFC and the IDA, and the three organizations share the same president, board of governors, and executive directors.

The bank is probably the world's biggest provider of financial assistance to developing economies. In fiscal year 2002 it provided over 100 developing nations with a total of $19.5 billion in loans, $11.5 through the IBRD and around $8.1 billion through the IDA. In 2002 the biggest share of new IBRD lending (some $4.9 billion) went to Europe and Central Asia, $4.2 billion went to Latin

The World Bank Group

The International Bank for Reconstruction and Development	The International Development Association	The International Finance Corporation	The Multilateral Investment Guarantee Agency	The International Center for Settlement of Investment Disputes
Established: 1945 Members: 184 Cumulative lending: $360 billion	Established: 1960 Members: 162 Cumulative lending: $135 billion	Established: 1956 Members: 175 Committed portfolio: $21.6 billion	Established: 1988 Members: 157 Cumulative guarantees issued: $10.34 billion	Established: 1966 Members: 134 Total cases registered: 103
Aims to reduce poverty in middle-income and creditworthy poor countries by promoting sustainable development through loans, guarantees, and nonlending services.	Provides interest-free credits to world's poorest countries.	Invests in sustainable private enterprises in developing countries; provides long-term loans and guarantees.	Encourages foreign investment in developing countries by providing loan guarantees.	Provides international facilities for conciliation and arbitration of investment disputes.

Source: World Bank, http://web.worldbank.org/ (March 20, 2003).

America and the Caribbean, and East Asia and the Pacific accounted for a further $1 billion. Membership of the bank is constantly growing. In 1982, for example, the bank had 142 members; by 2002 membership had reached 184.

World Bank Operations

In some ways, the bank works like an ordinary commercial bank. Its stated purpose is to make loans to developing economies; to make loans, it must have both capital and working funds. Capital is provided (subscribed) by member countries that contribute different amounts according to the relative strength of their economies. Members pay around 8.5 percent of their subscribed capital but must be ready to pay the remainder on request. The bank also generates working funds by offering bonds on the world's capital markets and by collecting interest and repayments on the loans it makes. The bank is virtually self-financing, earning almost as much money in interest and repayments as it grants in the form of loans; it has been profitable every year since its creation in 1946 and has never needed to call in the fully subscribed capital.

Unlike commercial banks making ordinary loans to private citizens, the World Bank takes a close interest in how members use its money. Usually (and sometimes in partnership with the IMF) it attaches stringent conditions to its loans ("conditionality"), requiring nations to adopt agreed economic development strategies known as Structural Adjustment Programs (SAPs), which have often proved intensely controversial. Money is generally provided only for specific projects for which borrowers have been unable to get loans in the commercial market at reasonable terms. World Bank loans have often been associated with massive infrastructure projects like hydroelectric power plants, highways, ports, pipelines, and airports, but most of the bank's loans are now made for agricultural and rural development projects. Money is lent both to member governments and to private companies operating in member states (governments must

Themes of World Bank Assistance 2001
• Accelerated debt relief to some of the world's poorest countries
• Improved development effectiveness
• Support for fight against HIV/AIDS
• Multidimensional support for poverty reduction:
• Emphasis on equal access to quality education
• Stress on cleaner, healthier environment
• Support for law reform:
• Legal education
• Anticorruption program in the judiciary
• Indigenous dispute resolution mechanisms
• Legal aid for poor women

Source: World Bank, http://web.worldbank.org/ (March 20, 2003).

guarantee the loans). Often the bank's staff provides technical as well as financial assistance with particular projects.

Since the 1980s the bank has focused much of its attention on projects that benefit the poorest people in the poorest nations; in 2002 part of its mission statement was "to fight poverty with passion and professionalism for lasting results." In the past the World Bank has frequently been criticized for imposing a one-size-fits-all development strategy on its borrowers, for example, by stipulating SAPs that prioritize debt repayment over public spending, require the privatization of public services, or force nations to grow cash crops for export rather than food for a sometimes undernourished home population. Largely as a response, the bank has developed a Comprehensive Development Framework in which each borrower country owns its own Poverty Reduction Strategy (a development plan to reduce poverty through macroeconomic, structural, and social policies), while the bank owns a parallel Country Assistance Strategy that determines how much financial and technical support it will provide. The bank continues to target its efforts at the poorest nations with task forces focusing on low- and middle-income nations. The high-profile Heavily Indebted Poor Countries (HIPC) Initiative, launched in 1996, aims to provide

A protester in the guise of World Bank president James Wolfensohn marches in the streets of Washington, D.C., on April 16, 2000, during anti-globalization protests.

relief for developing nations suffering most from the problems of long-term debt.

Issues and Controversies

Measuring the effectiveness of the World Bank's policies and programs—averaged over many different projects, across the entire developing world, over its half-century of existence—is difficult. The bank points to general gains in developing nations in areas like life expectancy (risen from 55 to 65 years), infant mortality (reduced by 50 percent), and adult literacy (doubled). Nevertheless, the bank readily acknowledges that considerable challenges remain.

The bank's policies have repeatedly been attacked by campaigners on environmental and Third World development issues. Critics charge that the bank, along with the IMF and a consortium of commercial banks, has knowingly perpetuated and exploited the Third World debt crisis for the overall financial benefit of the developed world in a throwback to colonial days. Environmental groups claim that the bank continues to finance what they maintain are environmentally suspect practices in developing nations, including growing crops with large amounts of agri-chemicals and pesticides, logging endangered forests, encouraging the use of fossil fuels, constructing massive highways and dams, and incinerating toxic waste. Critics have had some successes in challenging the World Bank. For example, in the 1990s the World Bank withdrew from a highly controversial plan to finance the Sardar Sarovar hydroelectric dam on India's Narmada River after finding itself the target of a worldwide environmental campaign. Further, the adjustment of the World Bank's one-size-fits-all policies is the result, in no small part, of pressure from opponents around the world.

The World Bank and its associated organizations will continue to play a definitive role in development for the foreseeable future. As the bank becomes increasingly sensitive to criticism, it is likely to adopt more strategies along the lines of the HIPC Initiative and to try to convince critics that its efforts are truly making a difference in world poverty. Whether its policies are an essential aid to economic development in poorer nations or sometimes contribute to the very problems they claim to relieve is likely to remain a matter of intense debate.

Further Reading

Caufield, Catherine. *Masters of Illusion: The World Bank and the Poverty of Nations.* New York: Henry Holt, 1996.

George, Susan. *A Fate Worse Than Debt.* New York: Grove Atlantic, 1990.

O'Brien, Robert, et al. *Contesting Global Governance: Multilateral Economic Institutions and Global Social Movements.* New York: Cambridge University Press, 2000.

World Bank Group. *Annual Report 2002.* Washington, D.C.: World Bank, 2002.

—*Chris Woodford*

World Trade Organization

The World Trade Organization (WTO) is an association based in Geneva, Switzerland, that seeks to liberalize and harmonize international trade restrictions for the economic benefit of its 144 member nations. Formed in 1995, the WTO is based on a set of agreements that grew out of the 1948 General Agreement on Tariffs and Trade (GATT); the GATT and the WTO agreements that supplement it effectively serve as the rule book for modern international commerce. The GATT was no more than an agreement between nations; the WTO, however, is an increasingly powerful—and controversial—international body with the same status as the International Monetary Fund (IMF) and the World Bank.

GATT and the WTO

During the Great Depression of the 1930s, many nations tried to help their economies by increasing exports and reducing imports, usually by imposing tariffs (taxes that made goods imported from other nations more expensive than equivalent goods produced at home) and quotas (restrictions on the amount of goods that could be imported). Known as protectionism, these actions led to a spiral of constantly escalating tariffs and other barriers that drastically reduced trade between nations and so worsened global economic conditions.

The solution involved a radical shift in the underlying principle of international trade away from protectionism and toward free trade (unimpeded by barriers like tariffs and quotas). Proposed at the United Nations (U.N.) Conference on Trade and Employment in 1947, this project took the form of the General Agreement on Tariffs and Trade, effective January 1948. The GATT was designed to reduce tariffs and other trade barriers among its 23 original contracting parties and to provide a mechanism for resolving trade disputes. The

GATT is based on two key principles: nondiscrimination and multilateralism. Nondiscrimination means that each member must treat all the other members equally by granting them most-favored-nation (MFN) status; if one member grants a special favor to another, for example, reducing tariffs, it must give equal treatment to all other members. Multilateralism means that trade can be carried out as easily across the globe as in a single domestic market.

Although the GATT was envisaged as a temporary arrangement that would lead to the creation of a formal U.N. trade watchdog—International Trade Organization (ITO)—political disagreements prevented the ITO from ever being established; instead the GATT was extended and refined during eight sets of trade negotiations (known as rounds) over the following 50 years. By the time of its final negotiations (the Uruguay Round) in 1993, the GATT had proven to be conspicuously successful, with tariffs on goods reduced to an average of 3.8 percent of their market value (compared with an average of 40 percent of their value in 1947). The GATT was also credited with bringing about a huge increase in global trade during the second half of the twentieth century by making the international trading system more stable and predictable. The growing importance and complexity of international trade, however, seemed to warrant a more extensive system of rules and a better system of resolving trade disputes between member nations. Just as the creation of the GATT had substantially increased world trade, the GATT's members argued, so would an even more extensive set of agreements produce even greater economic gains (later estimated by the WTO to be worth an annual increase in global trade of 12 percent or $745 billion).

Accordingly, the Uruguay Round discussed and implemented not just further reductions in tariffs and other nontariff barriers to trade but also an agreement to found a new and much more powerful body: the World Trade Organization, which

See also:
General Agreement on Tariffs and Trade; Globalization; International Trade; World Bank.

Albania *September 8, 2000*
Angola *November 23, 1996*
Antigua and Barbuda
January 1, 1995
Argentina *January 1, 1995*
Armenia *February 5, 2003*
Australia *January 1, 1995*
Austria *January 1, 1995*
Bahrain, Kingdom of
January 1, 1995
Bangladesh *January 1, 1995*
Barbados *January 1, 1995*
Belgium *January 1, 1995*
Belize *January 1, 1995*
Benin *February 22, 1996*
Bolivia *September 12, 1995*
Botswana *May 31, 1995*
Brazil *January 1, 1995*
Brunei Darussalam
January 1, 1995
Bulgaria *December 1, 1996*
Burkina Faso *June 3, 1995*
Burundi *July 23, 1995*
Cameroon
December 13, 1995
Canada *January 1, 1995*
Central African Republic
May 31, 1995
Chad *October 19, 1996*
Chile *January 1, 1995*
China *November 11, 2001*
Colombia *April 30, 1995*
Congo *March 27, 1997*
Costa Rica *January 1, 1995*
Côte d'Ivoire
January 1, 1995
Croatia *November 30, 2000*
Cuba *April 20, 1995*
Cyprus *July 30, 1995*
Czech Republic
January 1, 1995
Democratic Republic of the
Congo *January 1, 1997*
Denmark *January 1, 1995*
Djibouti *May 31, 1995*
Dominica *January 1, 1995*
Dominican Republic
March 9, 1995
Ecuador *January 21, 1996*
Egypt *June 30, 1995*
El Salvador *May 7, 1995*
Estonia *November 13, 1999*
European Communities
January 1, 1995

Fiji *January 14, 1996*
Finland *January 1, 1995*
France *January 1, 1995*
Gabon *January 1, 1995*
The Gambia
October 23, 1996
Georgia *June 14, 2000*
Germany *January 1, 1995*
Ghana *January 1, 1995*
Greece *January 1, 1995*
Grenada *February 22, 1996*
Guatemala *July 21, 1995*
Guinea *October 25, 1995*
Guinea-Bissau *May 31, 1995*
Guyana *January 1, 1995*
Haiti *January 30, 1996*
Honduras *January 1, 1995*
Hong Kong, China
January 1, 1995
Hungary *January 1, 1995*
Iceland *January 1, 1995*
India *January 1, 1995*
Indonesia *January 1, 1995*
Ireland *January 1, 1995*
Israel *April 21, 1995*
Italy *January 1, 1995*
Jamaica *March 9, 1995*
Japan *January 1, 1995*
Jordan *April 11, 2000*
Kenya *January 1, 1995*
Korea, Republic of
January 1, 1995
Kuwait *January 1, 1995*
Kyrgyz Republic
December 20, 1998
Latvia *February 10, 1999*
Lesotho *May 31, 1995*
Liechtenstein
September 1, 1995
Lithuania *May 31, 2001*
Luxembourg
January 1, 1995
Macao, China
January 1, 1995
Madagascar
November 17, 1995
Malawi *May 31, 1995*
Malaysia *January 1, 1995*
Maldives *May 31, 1995*
Mali *May 31, 1995*
Malta *January 1, 1995*
Mauritania *May 31, 1995*
Mauritius *January 1, 1995*
Mexico *January 1, 1995*

Moldova *July 26, 2001*
Mongolia *January 29,1997*
Morocco *January 1, 1995*
Mozambique
August 26, 1995
Myanmar *January 1, 1995*
Namibia *January 1, 1995*
Netherlands *January 1, 1995*
New Zealand
January 1, 1995
Nicaragua
September 3, 1995
Niger *December 13, 1996*
Nigeria *January 1, 1995*
Norway *January 1, 1995*
Oman *November 9, 2000*
Pakistan *January 1, 1995*
Panama *September 6, 1997*
Papua New Guinea
June 9, 1996
Paraguay *January 1, 1995*
Peru *January 1, 1995*
Philippines *January 1, 1995*
Poland *July 1, 1995*
Portugal *January 1, 1995*
Qatar *January 13, 1996*
Romania *January 1, 1995*
Rwanda *May 22, 1996*
Saint Kitts and Nevis
February 21, 1996
Saint Lucia *January 1, 1995*
Saint Vincent & the
Grenadines *January 1, 1995*
Senegal *January 1, 1995*
Sierra Leone *July 23, 1995*
Singapore *January 1, 1995*
Slovak Republic
January 1, 1995
Slovenia *July 30, 1995*
Solomon Islands
July 26, 1996
South Africa
January 1, 1995
Spain *January 1, 1995*
Sri Lanka *January 1, 1995*
Suriname *January 1, 1995*
Swaziland *January 1, 1995*
Sweden *January 1, 1995*
Switzerland *July 1, 1995*
Tanzania *January 1, 1995*
Taiwan (Separate Customs
Territory of Taiwan, Penghu,
Kinmen, and Matsu)
January 1, 2002

Thailand *January 1, 1995*
Togo *May 31, 1995*
Trinidad and Tobago
March 1, 1995
Tunisia *March 29, 1995*
Turkey *March 26, 1995*
Uganda *January 1, 1995*
United Arab Emirates
April 10, 1996
United Kingdom
January 1, 1995
United States of America
January 1, 1995
Uruguay *January 1, 1995*
Venezuela *January 1, 1995*
Zambia *January 1, 1995*
Zimbabwe *March 5, 1995*

Observer Status
Algeria
Andorra
Azerbaijan
Bahamas
Belarus
Bhutan
Bosnia and Herzegovina
Cambodia
Cape Verde
Equatorial Guinea
Ethiopia
Former Yugoslav Republic of
Macedonia
Holy See (Vatican)
Kazakhstan
Lao People's Democratic
Republic
Lebanese Republic
Nepal
Russian Federation
Samoa
São Tomé and Príncipe
Saudi Arabia
Serbia and Montenegro
Seychelles
Sudan
Tajikistan
Tonga
Ukraine
Uzbekistan
Vanuatu
Vietnam
Yemen

Source: World Bank home page, http:www.worldbank.org (March 20, 2003).

took over from the GATT on April 15, 1994. The WTO differs radically from the GATT in a number of ways. The GATT was simply an agreement between members overseen by a small staff; the WTO is a powerful international body with its own secretariat of 550 people. Where the GATT was an ad hoc and provisional agreement that was extended to compensate for the lack of an international trade organization, membership of the WTO is designed to be a permanent commitment.

The GATT was based on the traditional idea of international trade as an exchange of goods. However, the WTO covers several other forms of trade: the General Agreement in Trade and Services (GATS) extends the principles of free trade to service industries like finance and telecommunications; an agreement on Trade-Related Aspects of Intellectual Property Rights (TRIPs) expands patents and copyrights to give equal protection in all member nations. Agreements sometimes run into difficulties, but the WTO has a much more clearly defined and therefore quicker process for resolving trade disputes than had the GATT and more powerful disciplinary powers than U.N. organizations. Since the WTO superseded the GATT, membership has increased substantially: 125 nations signed the WTO's original agreements in 1995; by January 2002 membership had risen to 144 nations and many others had applied to join.

With its declared mission of helping trade to flow "smoothly, freely, fairly, and predictably," the WTO is effectively a clearinghouse for world trade issues where negotiations can be conducted, agreements can be administered, and disputes can be resolved. The WTO also reviews national trade policies, advises and provides expertise to developing countries on trading issues, and cooperates with a range of other international bodies. Although the WTO acts as the forum for international discussions on trade issues, all of its agreements (unlike those of the GATT) must be ratified in the national legislatures of member nations.

The nature of international trade is constantly changing; the WTO is constantly seeking to broaden the range of its agreements to cover other kinds of trade and to curb an increasing range of nontariff barriers. In 1997 members signed new agreements on the telecommunications sector; in 1998 they debated electronic commerce (e-commerce); and in 2000 they considered

China's foreign trade minister Shi Guangsheng signs the membership document at the ceremony marking China's entrance into the WTO in 2001.

Members of trade unions, farmers' organizations, and factory workers protest the WTO in New Delhi, India, in 2001.

agriculture and other services not previously covered by GATT or WTO agreements. Future WTO debates and agreements are expected to focus on a number of other controversial areas, including members' policies on international competition and the relationships between intellectual property and the protection of traditional rights, cultures, and the environment.

Debating the WTO

Reaching agreement on issues like these may prove problematic, but the WTO has been no stranger to controversy in its short history. WTO meetings have been a focus for sometimes violent protests by anti-globalization protesters. Critics level a variety of charges against the WTO, including the allegation that it pursues free trade at any cost by helping global commercial interests to gradually erode national environmental, health, and safety legislation for private profit. Another charge is that weaker nations, effectively forced to join the WTO because it controls more than 90 percent of world trade, find themselves powerless to shape the organization's policies once members. Critics claim that the WTO is undemocratic, dictatorial, and a tool of the world's most powerful transnational corporations and developed countries.

Responding to these charges, the WTO counters that all its decisions are negotiated openly and accountably and ratified by member governments; WTO policy, it claims, is dictated by member governments, not the reverse. As it exists to create a set of equitable rules for trade between its members, the WTO argues that it provides a defense against vested interests and a means for smaller countries to enjoy the same trading benefits as larger and more powerful ones. Although environmental protection and issues like health and safety are not the WTO's primary concern, it nevertheless argues that the removal of trade barriers, for example, agriculture and fishery subsidies, can bring considerable benefits to the global environment, while specific provisions in the GATT agreements allow governments to safeguard specific areas, provided the provisions are not used as hidden barriers to trade.

Together, the GATT and the WTO have contributed to a massive increase in global trade, estimated to be worth 14 times as much in 1997 as in 1950. The WTO claims that by reducing the trade barriers between nations and providing a clear mechanism for resolving disputes, it has led to a much more prosperous and peaceful world. As more nations apply to join the WTO and its agreements expand to cover even more aspects of international trade, the WTO seems certain to become both an increasingly powerful and increasingly controversial organization.

Further Reading

Bhagwati, Jagdish. *Free Trade Today.* Princeton, N.J.: Princeton University Press, 2002.

Nader, Ralph, et al. *The Case against Free Trade: GATT, NAFTA, and the Globalization of Corporate Power.* San Francisco: Earth Island Press, 1993.

Wallach, Lori, et al. *Whose Trade Organization?: Corporate Globalization and the Erosion of Democracy.* Washington, D.C.: Public Citizen, 1999.

World Trade Organization. *Trading into the Future.* Geneva: WTO, 2001.

—Chris Woodford

Xerox Corporation

Most company names are not listed in the dictionary as a verb. In the 1960s and 1970s the process of photocopying was associated so closely with one company—Xerox, the company that had invented plain paper photocopying—that the word *xerox* entered the language as a verb meaning to photocopy. Although Xerox is also responsible for many important developments in personal computing, the company remains known primarily for its creation of the photocopier.

Inventing the Copier

Before the creation of the photocopier, small-scale or personal copying was done on a mimeograph, a machine invented by Thomas Edison. The mimeograph was messy to use, its ink smelled bad, and, worst of all, it made poor copies. Larger jobs had to be done on offset printing presses, which were huge, expensive, and required an entire shop dedicated to their operation and maintenance.

In the 1930s Chester F. Carlson, a young physicist who had put himself through college at the California Institute of Technology, had a job working in the patent department of a New York electrical company. Part of his job was to retype manuscripts and send out drawings to photocopying firms. Frustrated by the high cost and slow pace of this process, Carlson began to spend his spare time working to create a machine that would copy documents at the push of a button.

In 1938 Carlson and his assistant, German physicist Otto Kornei, developed a way to copy documents using photoconductivity. Images were laid on a glass slide, then transferred to a metal plate by means of an electrical charge, a bright floodlight, and sulfur powder. The image on the metal plate was then transferred to a piece of waxed paper, producing the electrostatic copy.

Carlson perfected the process, obtained patents for it, and spent six years offering rights to the process to every important office equipment company in the country. He eventually sold the patent rights to the Battelle Development Corporation of Columbus, Ohio. In 1947 Haloid Company, a small firm that made photographic paper, bought the license to the patents from Battelle and changed the name of the process from electrophotography to xerography, from the Greek word *xeros*, meaning dry, and *graphein*, meaning writing. The word *Xerox* was trademarked the following year, and the first xerographic copier, the model A, was introduced in 1949. Difficult to operate, the model A was not a success; its copies came out on waxed paper, which was unsuitable for use in an office.

See also:
IBM; Research and Development; Technology; Total Quality Management.

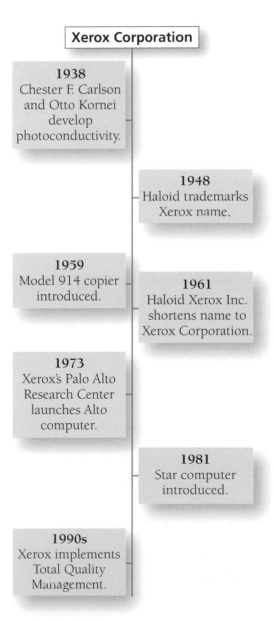

Xerox Corporation

1938
Chester F. Carlson and Otto Kornei develop photoconductivity.

1948
Haloid trademarks Xerox name.

1959
Model 914 copier introduced.

1961
Haloid Xerox Inc. shortens name to Xerox Corporation.

1973
Xerox's Palo Alto Research Center launches Alto computer.

1981
Star computer introduced.

1990s
Xerox implements Total Quality Management.

Chester Carlson with the first photocopier, circa 1950s.

patents on xerography from Battelle, giving the company a monopoly on the process; in 1961 Haloid Xerox Incorporated shortened its name to Xerox Corporation.

Shrinking the Computer

Throughout the 1960s Xerox's success and profits grew. However, the corporation's managers became concerned that they were banking everything on one product. Scientists were already beginning to think about the paperless office of the future—a paperless office that presumably would eliminate the need for copiers. Xerox executives decided that the company needed to diversify into the computer industry. After examining several computer companies, including Digital Equipment Corporation, Control Data, and Burroughs, Xerox acquired Scientific Data Systems (SDS) in 1969. Xerox paid a reported $900 million for the small micro-computer company, 92 times more than SDS's earnings at the time. The high price was an indicator of the importance Xerox placed on entering the computer business.

Xerox had always understood the critical role of research, and the company now opened a new research and development center focused on developing digital technology—the Palo Alto Research Center (PARC), formally created in 1970. The center was located in California, far from Xerox's New York headquarters, in the middle of the area that was about to become Silicon Valley, the high-tech capital of the world.

In the early 1970s computers were huge and extremely expensive. They were owned and used primarily by corporations and universities, and researchers had to fight each other to get enough time on the machines. PARC pioneered the then-revolutionary idea that computers should be small and affordable enough for each worker to have one—a personal computer. Its innovations, including multitasking and bit-mapped screens, allowed PARC to build smaller and cheaper products. The first prototype built by PARC was the Alto, completed in 1973. By the summer of 1974 the lab had 40 Altos and had designed the first local area network

For the next 10 years, Haloid poured money into the development of the xerography process with very limited success. In 1959 Haloid finally produced the model 914. Unlike the previous copiers, the 914 used plain paper and was simple to use; it operated at the push of a button, as Carlson had envisioned. The 914 was an instant success, and every office was soon equipped with a Haloid Xerox copier. That year, Haloid Xerox purchased all the worldwide

A demonstration of the Alto computer in the late 1970s.

(LAN), called Ethernet, to allow the computers to communicate with each other.

Along with the Alto, PARC researchers developed supporting software and hardware, such as the laser printer; the mouse; WYSIWYG (What You See Is What You Get) word processing, which allowed a document to appear on the monitor screen the way it would look when printed; and a graphical user interface that was demonstrated for Steve Jobs and later became the basis for the Macintosh computers.

Although the Alto was more advanced than anything else on the market, Xerox had financial problems that led it to turn away from marketing the personal computer. The Federal Trade Commission (FTC) had filed a complaint against Xerox in 1972, charging it with restraint of trade and illegally monopolizing the copier industry. More antitrust lawsuits against Xerox followed from IBM and other companies. During the 1970s Xerox became known as the most-sued company in America.

Although the lawsuits were eventually settled, the settlement and legal costs created pressure at Xerox to develop a new product that could be marketed immediately. The Xerox research facility in Dallas had developed a dedicated word processor that could be produced more cheaply and quickly than the Alto. In what is considered one of the great lost opportunities in the history of American business, Xerox scrapped the Alto and threw its efforts into marketing word processors instead. Just a few years later, the widespread popularity of personal computers would destroy the market for word processors forever.

After a great deal of internal fighting, PARC convinced Xerox to develop a personal computing system, the Star. The Star was the first computer system to use pictures (icons), lists of action choices (menus), and multiple

They [Xerox PARC researchers] showed me really three things. But I was so blinded by the first one I didn't even really see the other two. One of the things they showed me was object-oriented programming; they showed me that, but I didn't even see that. The other one they showed me was a networked computer system. They had over a hundred Alto computers all networked using e-mail etc., etc. I didn't even see that. I was so blinded by the first thing they showed me, which was the graphical user interface. I thought it was the best thing I'd ever seen in my life . . . and within, you know, 10 minutes it was obvious to me that all computers would work like this some day. . . .

Basically they [the Xerox executives] were copier heads that just had no clue about a computer or what it could do. And so they just grabbed defeat from the greatest victory in the computer industry. Xerox could have owned the entire computer industry today. Could have been, you know, a company 10 times its size. Could have been IBM—could have been the IBM of the nineties. Could have been the Microsoft of the nineties.

—-Steve Jobs, *Triumph of the Nerds* (television documentary), 1996

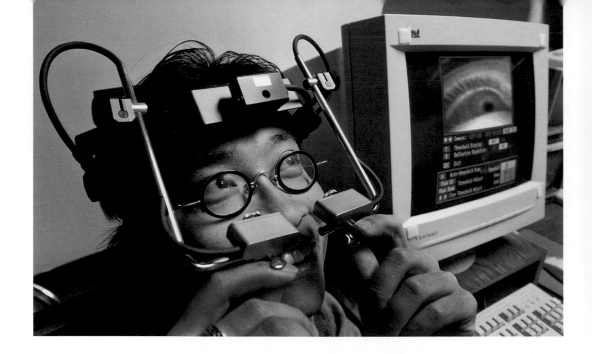

In 2001, a Xerox PARC scientist demonstrates a head-mounted tracking device that can record the focus of a user's attention as he looks at Web pages.

screen sections (windows) that were designed to electronically represent parts of a typical office like the desktop, file cabinet, telephone, in and out boxes, wastepaper basket, and so on. The Star was also the first personal computing system to incorporate a bit-map screen, a mouse, high-quality laser printing, WYSIWYG word processing, Ethernet, and software that could combine text and graphics in the same document. However, by the time the Star was introduced in April 1981, the market was already full of alternate systems.

The Star also had flaws. The system was expensive and operated very slowly. Although marketed to executives, it did not include spreadsheet software. It was not compatible with other computers; Xerox would not release its programming language to the public; and Xerox copier salespeople received little training on the computers and did not understand them. Just as Xerox was finally marketing the Star, IBM released the IBM PC. Within a few years, Xerox pulled out of the market and sold SDS.

Back to Basics

Following its disastrous experiences with personal computers, Xerox decided to concentrate on its original photocopier business. The company adopted a new Japanese management idea, Total Quality Management. With this emphasis on reliability, Xerox managed to wrest back some of the market share in copiers it had lost during its foray into word processing and personal computers.

In the early 1990s Xerox began transforming its copiers into more versatile pieces of equipment capable of sending documents and graphics to computers and over facsimile machines and capable of electronically linking scores of workstations together. Xerox has also continued to lead in the development and marketing of the laser printer and the flat panel display screen, both developed at PARC. However, the management style that led to the personal computer disaster continued to plague the company through the 1990s, and the future of Xerox may rest as much on adopting new styles of management as on developing new copier technology.

Further Reading

Dorsey, David. *The Force.* New York: Random House, 1994.

Gabor, Andrea. *The Man Who Discovered Quality.* New York: Times Books, 1990.

Hiltzick, Michael. *Dealers of Lightning: Xerox PARC and the Dawn of the Computer Age.* New York: HarperBusiness, 1999.

Kearns, David T., and David A. Nadler. *Prophets in the Dark.* New York: HarperBusiness, 1992.

Saffo, Paul. "The Alto: Today's Technology Yesterday." *Personal Computing,* June 1989.

Smith, Douglas K., et al. *Fumbling the Future.* Lincoln, Neb.: iUniverse, 1990.

—Lisa Magloff

Yahoo!

Yahoo! is a Web portal, a site that helps Internet users find their way around the World Wide Web. Yahoo! features a search engine and directory that links to millions of other Web sites. With more than 200 million users each month, Yahoo! has become the premier Web portal, but the short history of Yahoo! illustrates another aspect of the Internet boom: how to keep the money coming in when there is nothing to sell. As Yahoo! grappled with that issue, it abandoned some of the principles that led to its success. Yahoo!'s history in many ways mirrors that of the Web.

Yahoo! began as a hobby. The founders, David Filo and Jerry Yang, were doctoral candidates in electrical engineering at Stanford University. Awareness of the World Wide Web was beginning to spread, especially among college students. At the start of 1994, Filo and Yang began making a list of their favorite Internet Web sites. Eventually their lists became too long and unwieldy, and they broke them out into categories. When the categories became too full, they developed subcategories. This arrangement of information is called a hierarchical list, and it is the core concept of Yahoo!

Soon, Filo and Yang were spending more time on compiling their lists of favorite links than on their doctoral dissertations. They put their hierarchically organized lists onto a Web site of their own, originally called, "Jerry's Guide to the World Wide Web." The name was soon changed to Yahoo!, supposedly an acronym for "Yet Another Hierarchical Officious Oracle." Filo and Yang later confessed that their fondness for the name had more to do with the dictionary definition of *yahoo*—unsophisticated and uncouth.

The Big Time

The Web site soon developed a loyal following. Users would e-mail Filo and Wang with suggestions on how to improve the site. Yahoo! had its first million-hit day in the fall of 1994, representing about 100,000 individual visitors.

In March 1995 Yang and Filo incorporated their business and lined up financing through Sequoia Capital, the venture capital firm that had funded Apple Computer, Atari, Oracle, and Cisco Systems. Sequoia's initial investment in Yahoo! was nearly $2 million. At the same time, Netscape was persuaded to place Yahoo! on its Net directory, increasing the number of hits to 10 million per week. A professional management team was brought on board, and a second round of funding was secured in the fall of 1995 from Reuters and the venture capital firm Softbank. Yahoo! made its first profit—$92,000—in the fourth quarter of 1995.

Yahoo! grew very quickly, partly because venture capital to fund Internet search engines in the mid-1990s was plentiful and partly because Yahoo! had a huge base of loyal users. Many users were originally attracted to Yahoo! because they felt the site

Yahoo!

1994
David Filo and Jerry Yang found Yahoo!

1994
In the fall, Yahoo! has its first million-hit day.

1995
Yang and Filo incorporate their business, receiving funding from a venture capital firm.

2001
Yahoo!'s stock falls to $16 a share from a high of $237.

2001
Slightly more than half of the Internet's entire population uses Yahoo!

See also:
E-Business; Information Revolution; Internet.

Cofounders of Yahoo!, David Filo and Jerry Yang, in 1998.

represented the grassroots origins of the Internet: the site operated using free software and listed every Web page it could find, no matter how small. Other sites loaded up their home pages with huge advertisements; Yahoo! kept ads simple and catered to the home user with a slow Internet connection. Yahoo! developed an image as a portal free from commercial influence.

Nevertheless, Yahoo! still had to make money. Like many other Web sites, Yahoo! planned to earn revenues from advertising. The company bought popular small Web sites, including the free home pages of GeoCities and eGroups' mailing lists to build an ever-larger audience and charge higher advertising rates. Yahoo! rapidly became a large corporation.

Facing Reality

In the late 1990s the technology bubble burst, and Internet advertising dried up. Yahoo! was hit hard. By the start of 2001, the company's stock had fallen to around $16 per share from a high of $237.

Yahoo! had introduced a service earlier that allowed businesses to pay a fee to ensure a speedy listing on the portal. Yahoo! began selling prominent placement on its directory pages. The company also offered premium services, in which users are charged for extras like games, music services, and personal ads. These actions led to criticism from some users who claim the company gives its partners, including Mapquest and Reuters, more prominent listings than competing sites. They argue that having one company both classifying Net services and providing them is a conflict of interest. Critics have also complained that Yahoo! no longer lists every site it can find but instead focuses on corporate sites and those that pay to be listed.

According to Nielsen/NetRatings, in October 2001 slightly more than half of the Internet's entire population used Yahoo! Yet advertising revenues in 2001 had fallen by 10 percent from the previous year. Yahoo! may find that future profits will depend less on advertising revenue and more on charging for premium services. Casting Yahoo! as an idealist that abandoned its principles when faced with the harsh realities of competition is easy. However, the way Yahoo! addresses the problem of how to turn a profit on the Internet may point the way for the future of e-business.

Further Reading

Angel, Karen. *Inside Yahoo!: Reinvention for the Road Ahead*. New York: John Wiley & Sons, 2002.

Towers, J. Tarin, ed. *Yahoo! Wild Web Rides*. Foster City, Calif.: IDG Books, 1996.

Vlamis, Anthony, and Bob Smith. *Do You? Business the Yahoo! Way*. Milford, Conn.: Capstone Publications, 2002.

—*Lisa Magloff*

Yamaha Corporation

Yamaha fused Japanese business models with Western products to grow from a small business into a global leader. Subsidiaries located in foreign countries used local labor and materials but were organized and run using Japanese business models. Organizational integration, along with an emphasis on research and development, allowed Yamaha to innovate and adapt products like the piano and the motorcycle, making them both cheaper and better and turning Yamaha into a global company.

Tuning Up

Yamaha has had a reputation for quality and craftsmanship since its founding. The company was started in 1887 by Torakusu Yamaha (1851–1917), an instrument maker who had set out to build high-quality reed organs. At that time, Western styles and ideas were just becoming fashionable in Japan. Yamaha realized that a craze for Western instruments might soon develop, and he applied traditional Japanese craftsmanship to build Japan's first reed organ. Pianos and other Western instruments did indeed become popular in Japan, and after 10 years of growth Yamaha joined with other businessmen in 1897 to found the Nippon Gakki Company (Japanese Musical Instrument Company). Yamaha was named company president. Over the next 20 years, Nippon Gakki earned a reputation throughout the music world for high-quality pianos and organs. A Yamaha piano and a Yamaha organ both received honorary grand prize at the 1904 St. Louis World's Fair.

The company grew steadily during the first half of the twentieth century, adding more and more musical instruments, pipe organs and guitars among them, to its line. During World War II, Yamaha switched its production to war goods. After the war, Yamaha's fourth president, Gen-ichi Kawakami, decided to use what was left of the company's wartime production machinery to set up a production line for a new product: motorcycles. In 1954 production of the first motorcycles began, a simple 125cc single-cylinder machine that copied the well-known German DKW design. (The British BSA Company also copied the German DKW in the postwar era and manufactured it as the Bantam.)

Although Yamaha would first sell motorcycles primarily within Asia, the company's ability to adapt new technology quickly and cheaply turned Yamaha Motors into the second largest manufacturer of motorcycles in the world. Yamaha Motor Corporation is

See also:
Globalization; Innovation.

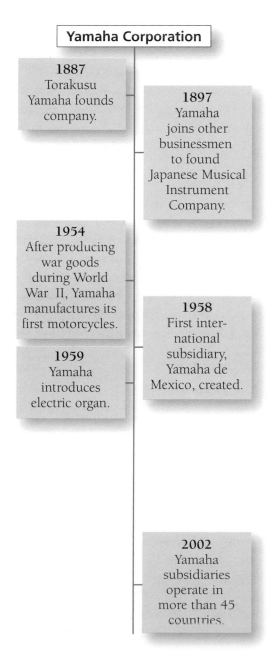

Yamaha Corporation

1887 Torakusu Yamaha founds company.

1897 Yamaha joins other businessmen to found Japanese Musical Instrument Company.

1954 After producing war goods during World War II, Yamaha manufactures its first motorcycles.

1958 First international subsidiary, Yamaha de Mexico, created.

1959 Yamaha introduces electric organ.

2002 Yamaha subsidiaries operate in more than 45 countries.

Yamaha employees demonstrate the "virtual piano school" system in Tokyo in 2000. An electric piano, a computer, and video cameras are integrated to enable a long-distance piano lesson.

a separately managed business entity and a partly owned subsidiary of the Yamaha Corporation. Yamaha Corporation owns about 28 percent of Yamaha Motors.

Going Global

During the 1950s and 1960s, Yamaha began expanding into the manufacture of other goods. The company's first overseas subsidiary, Yamaha de Mexico, was set up in 1958, and other overseas subsidiaries soon followed. Yamaha's largest subsidiary, Yamaha International Corporation, U.S., was established in 1960. By 2002 Yamaha subsidiaries were operating in more than 45 countries.

Yamaha also opened its own chain of music schools. Begun in 1954 to promote Western musical styles in Japan, Yamaha Music Schools spread rapidly around the world. By teaching music using Yamaha instruments, whole generations of schoolchildren were introduced to Yamaha. Since 1987 Yamaha has also operated international English-language schools in which teaching is based on English-language songs.

Yamaha first went electric in 1954, when it began marketing hi-fi players. Yamaha became popular among a whole

new group of musicians when it introduced the electronic organ, the Electone, in 1959. The electronic keyboard was not only much smaller and cheaper than the piano, it was also easier to use. Portable keyboards, synthesizers, and computer music equipment followed. In the 1990s Yamaha began developing "silent instruments"—instruments that can be listened to through headphones, to spare neighbors and family from having to listen to drum practice.

Much of Yamaha's success can be traced to its diversification strategy. The company has, for the most part, stuck to areas involving recreation: instruments and audiovisual equipment, skis, archery, motorcycling, snowmobiles, golf carts, outboard engines, water vehicles, and resorts. Yamaha has also begun branching out into semiconductors and other computer-related products, home appliances and furniture, specialty metals, machine tools, and industrial robots. Yamaha Motors manufactures unmanned industrial helicopters for crop spraying, electro-hybrid bicycles, generators, and auto and boat motors. Its diverse product line has protected Yamaha against recessions and market downturns. In addition, an emphasis on hierarchy and loyalty gave Yamaha a devoted workforce and stable management—the company had just seven presidents in its first 100 years.

Further Reading

Ide, Masasuke. *Japanese Corporate Finance and International Competition: Japanese Capitalism Versus American Capitalism.* New York: St. Martin's, 1998.

Kester, Carl W. *Japanese Takeovers: The Global Contest for Corporate Control.* Boston: Harvard Business School Press, 1991.

Macauley, Ted. *The Yamaha Legend.* New York: St. Martin's Press, 1979.

Nonaka, Ikujiro, et al. *The Knowledge-Creating Company: How Japanese Companies Create the Dynamics of Innovation.* New York: Oxford University Press, 1995.

Ohmae, Kenichi. *The Mind of the Strategist: The Art of Japanese Business.* New York: McGraw-Hill Professional Publishing, 1991.

—*Lisa Magloff*

Glossary

asset management Process of managing money and other items of value to make them grow in value.

blue chip Well-established company (or the stock of such company) considered to be a leader in its industry; Microsoft is a blue chip computer company.

bondholders Individuals or entities that own bonds.

bonds Certificates stating that a firm or government will pay the holder regular interest payments and a set sum on a specific maturity date. See encyclopedia entry, Stocks and Bonds.

brand equity Value represented by a consumer's preference for a specific company's good or service. See encyclopedia entry, Brand Names.

capital Money or wealth that is put at risk to fund a business enterprise. See encyclopedia entry.

Chapter 11 bankruptcy Legal proceeding that permits a business to continue to operate while restructuring finances and paying creditors. See encyclopedia entry, Bankruptcy.

conglomerate A company that grows by merging with or buying businesses in several different industries.

day laborer Workers without permanent employment who work one day for a set wage; many farm workers are day laborers. See encyclopedia entry, Temporary Workers.

demand Amount of a good or service consumers will purchase at different prices at a given time.

entrepreneur Person who combines different resources to make goods or services available to others. See encyclopedia entry, Entrepreneurship.

fair market value Price at which property would change hands between a willing buyer and a willing seller when both are fully informed about the asset.

incubator Private or publicly funded entity that provides facilities and support staff for small businesses.

independent contractor Self-employed person who offers services to the public. See encyclopedia entry, Freelancing.

investment bank Financial entity that provides expertise in assisting companies selling stock to the public.

joint-stock bank Group of individuals who pool their money in order to invest.

just-in-time Use of sophisticated computer inventory tracking software to lower business costs by minimizing inventory held and delivery times; both manufacturing and retail businesses use the technique. See encyclopedia entry, Just-in-Time Inventory.

laissez-faire Doctrine that the government should not interfere in the economy.

liberalism In economics, the belief that a nation's wealth can achieve greatest increase by ensuring minimum government interference with trade.

liquidity event Conversion of a company into liquid assets like stock or cash.

market share Percentage of all dollars spent on a product or service that a specific company earns for that product or service; the proportion of a particular market dominated by a specific company.

minority interest Any share of ownership that is less than 50 percent.

monopoly Type of market that involves only one seller. See encyclopedia entry.

monopsony Market with a single buyer of a good or service.

productivity Amount of work that can be completed in a given time. See encyclopedia entry.

prototype Working model of a product. See encyclopedia entry, Patent.

rationalism Belief that reason is the only means to pursue progress for humanity.

retail Sellers of goods and services to the general public. See encyclopedia entry, Retail and Wholesale.

royalty Payment made for the use of a resource—usually intellectual property. See encyclopedia entry, Intellectual Property.

stock options Right of employees (granted by employer) to buy shares in a company at a certain price at some point in the future.

subsidiary A business controlled by another business.

supply Amount of a good or service producers will provide at different prices at a given time.

sweatshop Production facilities with poor working conditions and low pay.

time value of money Money loses value over time; $1 of income today is more valuable than $1 of income five years from now.

total quality management (TQM) Body of organizational and business theories and techniques that focus on ways to provide high-quality products and services. See encyclopedia entry.

trademark Legal ownership of a unique symbol or design associated with a product or service. See encyclopedia entry.

unemployment rate Percentage of people in the labor force who are willing to work but are not employed. See encyclopedia entry, Unemployment.

working conditions Term encompassing a wide variety of on-the-job concerns, including worker safety, hours, benefits, and discrimination. See encyclopedia entry.

Index

Page numbers in **boldface** type indicate article titles. Page numbers in *italic* type indicate illustrations or other graphics.